BOOK COOKS

26 Recipes from A-Z Inspired by Favorite Children's Books

P9-DIJ-192

Written by
Cheryl Apgar

Editor: Sheri Samoiloff
Illustrator: Darcy Tom
Cover Illustrator: Rick Grayson
Designer: Mary Gagné
Cover Designer: Barbara Peterson
Art Director: Tom Cochrane
Project Director: Carolea Williams

Table of Contents

Introduction

Stir up a batch of eager learners with the skills-based activities in *Book Cooks*. The 26 easy-to-follow recipes—one for each letter of the alphabet—and numerous activities enhance literacy and math skills while motivating young learners and involving them in enjoyable, hands-on cooking experiences.

The easy-to-follow recipes require very little preparation, and only two recipes require a heat source. As your young chefs cook up fun food creations, they will also practice valuable math skills such as measuring, counting, patterning, identifying shapes, and making fractions.

Each "tasty" theme uses a popular children's book to introduce the theme and tie together the skills-based cooking experience with literature. Also included is a simple list of ingredients; step-by-step directions; reproducible student recipe cards; literature links; a related poem, chant, or song; and two activity ideas. Read the recommended books to the class throughout the week to reinforce the theme. Use the playful verses in the poem, chant, or song to help children practice identifying rhyming words, capital letters, and punctuation marks. Enhance the cooking experiences with the related activities that encourage children to write, graph, sort by shape or size, solve math problems, and create colorful art projects. Strengthen the home–school connection by creating individual cookbooks that children can take home with all the recipes from this resource.

This all-in-one resource is designed to make cooking a breeze. Children will practice valuable skills while munching on delicious goodies. Bon appetit!

Using This Book

Each "tasty" theme contains the same components. This sample guideline of how to implement a week-long theme can be applied to any theme from this resource.

Getting Organized

At the beginning of the year, send home with each child the Classroom Chefs parent letter (page 7) that asks volunteers to donate ingredients. At the beginning of each week, choose the theme of study. Review the recipe, and gather the utensils and supplies needed. Copy the Chef's Helper letter (page 8), and list the ingredients. Send the letter home to a volunteer who has agreed to purchase ingredients.

Introducing Literature

Begin each theme by reviewing the related literature synopsis. Read aloud the book, and discuss with the class how the book relates to the theme of study for the week. Read aloud throughout the week additional books from the related literature list.

Learning the Poem, Chant, or Song

Next, copy the poem, chant, or song onto an overhead transparency, chart paper, or sentence strips. For easy reference, use a different color of ink for each line. Point to each word, and have children echo each word as you say it. Underline the rhyming words, encourage children to identify them, and have children tap the words in rhythm. Have children identify and circle each capital letter. Have children identify and draw a triangle around each punctuation mark. Reintroduce the poem, chant, or song throughout the week until children have memorized it.

Teaching the Activities

After reading the related book and introducing the poem, chant, or song for the week, have children complete the activities. The required materials for each activity are in boldfaced type the first time each material is mentioned to help you identify needed materials at a glance. (Lined paper, pencils, scissors, crayons, markers, and glue are assumed to be readily available and are not in bold.)

Creating and Introducing the Cooking Center

As a culminating activity, have children make the recipe of the week. To prepare for this, choose a location in your classroom for the cooking center. Place the center near a sink, if possible. Set up all the utensils and supplies for the recipe of the week. Copy and cut apart the reproducible recipe cards. Place on the table the cards along with the ingredients in the order they will be used. Show the utensils, supplies, ingredients, and recipe to children. Have children make the recipe individually or in small groups (multiply the ingredients by the number of children in the group). Ask a parent volunteer to help children measure and cut ingredients and answer any questions children might have while they are cooking.

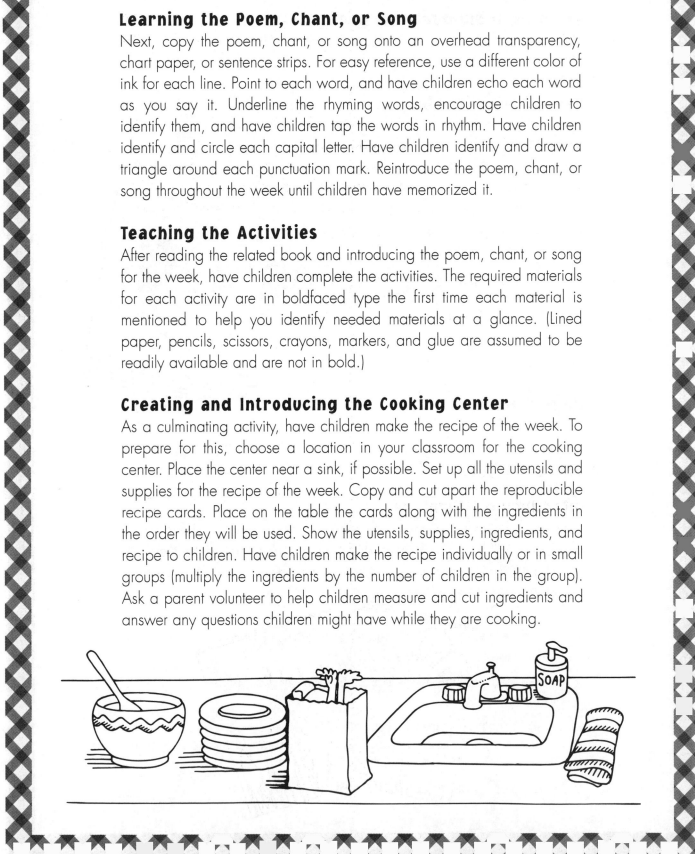

Creating Individual Cookbooks

Write each child's name on a separate file folder. After the class completes a recipe, give each child a copy of the corresponding page with the recipe, directions, and poem/song/chant. Invite children to comment on the recipe by drawing a happy or sad face in the *I think this recipe is* box at the top of the page. Collect the papers, and store them in the file folders. Copy a class set of the student cookbook cover reproducible (page 9). Give each child a copy of the reproducible, and have children decorate their cookbook cover. When the class has completed all the recipes, bind together each child's 26 recipe pages and completed cookbook cover; or glue each child's cover to his or her file folder, and staple together the pages to create individual cookbooks. Invite children to take home their cookbook and share the recipes with their family.

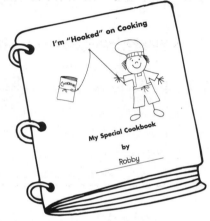

Helpful Hints

Use these helpful hints for a successful cooking experience.

✓ Check every child's record for food allergies. Substitute ingredients when necessary.

✓ Consider using reusable tableware instead of paper. While it requires washing, it is less expensive and more environmentally friendly.

✓ Discuss safety with the class. Only allow adults to use utensils with sharp edges.

✓ Explain appropriate behavior and fair consequences when working at the cooking center.

✓ If possible, set up the cooking center near a sink and away from other activity areas.

✓ Have parent volunteers help you prepare and supervise the cooking activities.

✓ Enlist the help of parents to shop for ingredients each week. Use the Classroom Chefs letter (page 7) at the beginning of the year and the Chef's Helper letter (page 8) as a reminder each week.

✓ Immediately wipe up any spills to avoid slippery floors.

Classroom Chefs

Dear Parents,

Our class is using cooking to enhance learning. Please help us by volunteering to provide food for one of our recipes. At the end of the year, your child will bring home a cookbook with all the recipes we have made this year. Enjoy watching your child's self-esteem soar when he or she prepares a recipe for family and friends.

Thank you for your help!

Sincerely,

- -
Please return the bottom portion of this letter to your child's teacher.

Yes, I would like to help by providing ingredients.

_____

Name & Phone Number

Sorry, I am unavailable at this time.

_____

Name

Chef's Helper

Dear_____,

Thank you for offering to provide the ingredients for this week's cooking experience. We will be cooking on _____, and we will need the following ingredients:

_____   _____

_____   _____

_____   _____

_____   _____

Please drop off these ingredients at our classroom on or before_____.

Sincerely,

Book Cooks © 2002 Creative Teaching Press

I'm "Hooked" on Cooking

My Special Cookbook

by

_____

Apple Smile

Johnny Appleseed

by Steven Kellogg (William Morrow & Company)

Children will love learning about John Chapman, one of the most gentle and generous of America's historical figures. Noted for his love of nature, he lived with the people who befriended him on his journey west. He planted apple seeds that supplied pioneer families with apple trees and earned him the name Johnny Appleseed.

Children will get a "taste" of Johnny Appleseed's life by learning about the different ways to eat apples and sort seeds. Children will love showing off their delicious "apple smiles."

Activity Apple Graph

Activity Seed Sorting

Song "Little Johnny Appleseed"

Cooking Experience Apple Smile

Related Literature

The Apple Pie Tree by Zoe Hall (Scholastic)
The Seasons of Arnold's Apple Tree by Gail Gibbons (Harcourt)
Ten Apples Up On Top! by Dr. Seuss (Random House)

Apple Smile

Math Skill
- counting by 1s

Name _____

I think this recipe is

Recipe

Ingredients
- 1 apple
- 1 teaspoon peanut butter or frosting
- 5 mini-marshmallows

Utensils and Supplies
- sharp knife (adult use only)
- plastic knife
- measuring spoon
- paper plate

Ask an adult to cut an apple into thin wedges and remove the apple core. Spread 1 teaspoon peanut butter or frosting on one side of two separate apple wedges. Place five mini-marshmallows between the apple wedges to make "teeth." Eat the apple wedges, and smile.

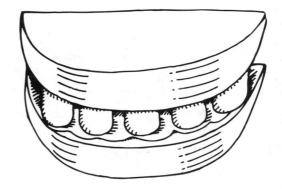

Little Johnny Appleseed
(to the tune of "Down by the Station")

Little Johnny Appleseed
Has a great big smile.
Big lips, big teeth . . .
You'll see it for a mile.

I wonder what his secret is?
He's looking rather sly.
Yes, Little Johnny Appleseed
Is quite a funny guy.

Apple Smile Recipe Cards

1. Spread 1 teaspoon peanut butter or frosting on one side of each apple wedge.

2. Place five mini-marshmallows on one of the wedges to make "teeth."

3. Put the apple wedges together.

4. Take a bite, and smile.

Apple Smile

Apple Graph

Draw on **chart paper** a graph with four columns. Label the columns *Apple, Applesauce, Candied Apple,* and *Apple Pie,* and draw corresponding pictures. Title the graph *How Do You Like Your Apples?* Write each child's name on a separate **apple-shaped die-cut,** and place **tape** on the back of the die-cuts. Ask children to place their die-cut on the graph to show their favorite way to eat an apple.

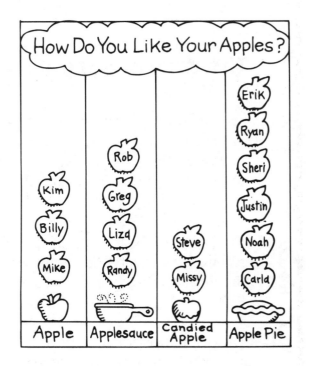

Seed Sorting

Give each child a **variety of seeds** and a piece of **blank paper or cardboard.** Ask children to sort their seeds by common attributes. Then, have them glue each group of seeds to their paper. Write the names of the seeds on the chalkboard, and have children label the groups on their paper. Invite children to share their completed seed sort with the class.

Beautiful Butterfly

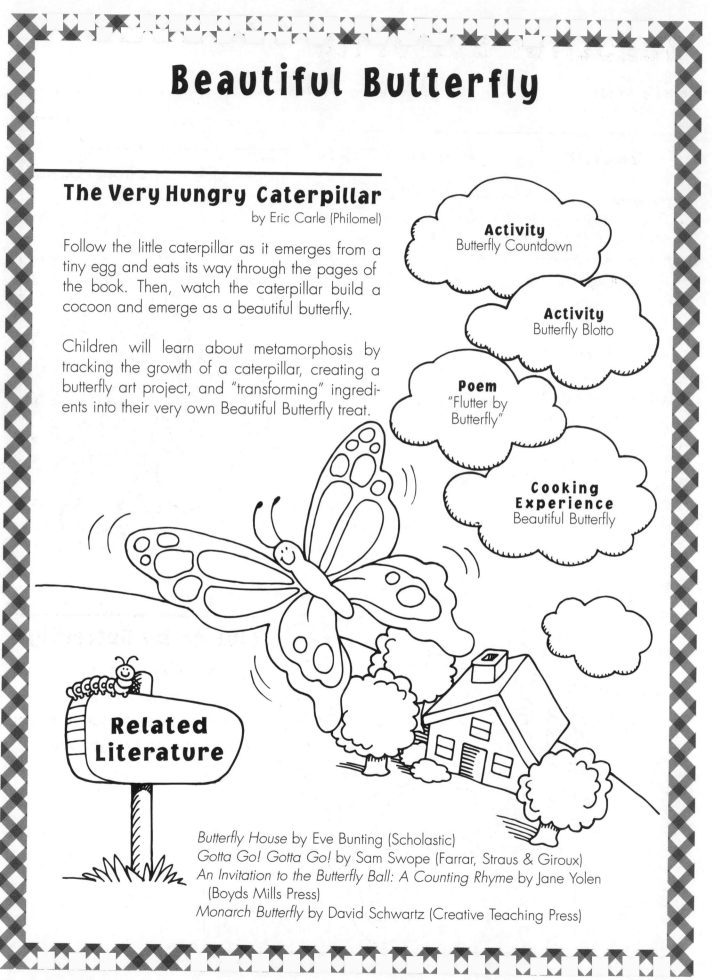

The Very Hungry Caterpillar
by Eric Carle (Philomel)

Follow the little caterpillar as it emerges from a tiny egg and eats its way through the pages of the book. Then, watch the caterpillar build a cocoon and emerge as a beautiful butterfly.

Children will learn about metamorphosis by tracking the growth of a caterpillar, creating a butterfly art project, and "transforming" ingredients into their very own Beautiful Butterfly treat.

Activity
Butterfly Countdown

Activity
Butterfly Blotto

Poem
"Flutter by Butterfly"

Cooking Experience
Beautiful Butterfly

Related Literature

Butterfly House by Eve Bunting (Scholastic)
Gotta Go! Gotta Go! by Sam Swope (Farrar, Straus & Giroux)
An Invitation to the Butterfly Ball: A Counting Rhyme by Jane Yolen
  (Boyds Mills Press)
Monarch Butterfly by David Schwartz (Creative Teaching Press)

Beautiful Butterfly

Math Skill
• counting by 2s

Name _____

I think this recipe is ⬜

Recipe

Ingredients
• 1 celery stalk
• 1 tablespoon softened cream cheese
• 2 pretzel twists
• 2 raisins
• 2 black licorice strings

Utensils and Supplies
• plastic knife
• measuring spoon
• paper plate

Wash one celery stalk, and cut it into a 4" (10 cm) piece. Fill the center of the celery with 1 tablespoon softened cream cheese. Add two pretzels to make "wings." Add two raisins to make "eyes" and two 1" (2.5 cm) pieces of black licorice strings to make "antennae."

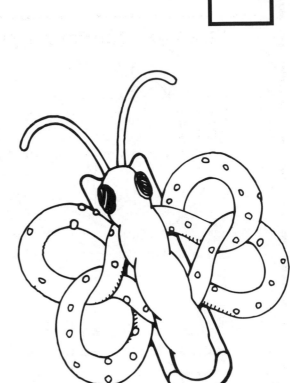

Flutter by Butterfly

Butterfly, as you flutter by,
Won't you think of me?
Then come and whisper in my ear
And tell me 'bout all you see.

Beautiful Butterfly Recipe Cards

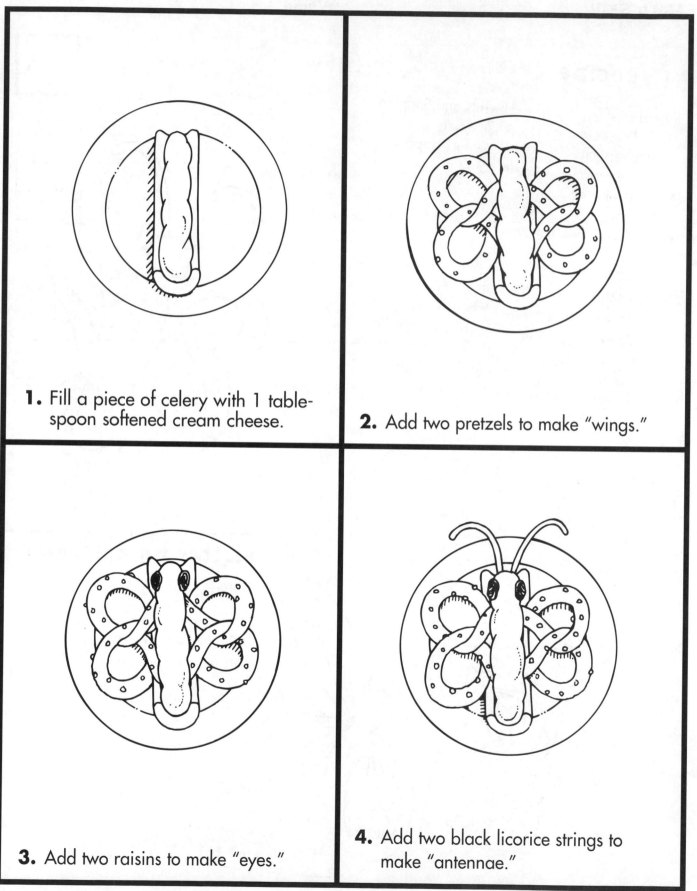

1. Fill a piece of celery with 1 table-spoon softened cream cheese.

2. Add two pretzels to make "wings."

3. Add two raisins to make "eyes."

4. Add two black licorice strings to make "antennae."

Book Cooks © 2002 Creative Teaching Press

Beautiful Butterfly

Butterfly Countdown

In advance, order **caterpillars** from a science supply store. Once they arrive, use the enclosed directions for feed and care. Use a **calendar** to predict when the caterpillars will make their chrysalis and when they will emerge as butterflies. Use the calendar to track their growth and record any changes. Once the butterflies have emerged, have a farewell party, and set them free outside. To extend the activity, show children a map, and discuss the places where the butterflies might fly.

SUN.	MON.	TUES.	WED.	THURS.	FRI.	SAT.
1	2	3 Larvae arrive	4	5	6	7
8	9	10	11 pupas ?	12	13	14
15	16	17	18	19	20	21
22	23	24 Adults?	25	26	27	28
29	30					

April

Butterfly Blotto

Give each child a **Butterfly Blotto reproducible (page 18)**, **tempera paint,** and a **paintbrush.** Ask children what they see on the reproducible (e.g., caterpillar, leaves). Explain to the class that when they fold their paper, cut around the picture, and then open it, they will discover something new. Ask them to predict what they will see once they cut out their picture. Have children color the caterpillar and leaves and then fold their paper on the dotted lines. Have them open their paper, turn the blank side faceup, and paint bright colors on the right side of their paper. Tell children to refold their paper and press it together. Have them reopen their paper to let the paint dry. Then, have children fold the paper so the printed side is showing and cut around the caterpillar and the leaves. Have children reopen their paper to discover the painted butterfly they created. Glue the center and the edges of each butterfly on a contrasting piece of **construction paper** to create a three-dimensional picture. Select a **butterfly poem,** and have children write it below their butterfly.

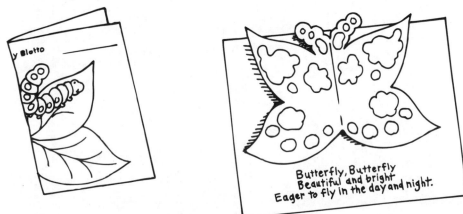

Butterfly, Butterfly
Beautiful and bright
Eager to fly in the day and night.

Butterfly Blotto

Name

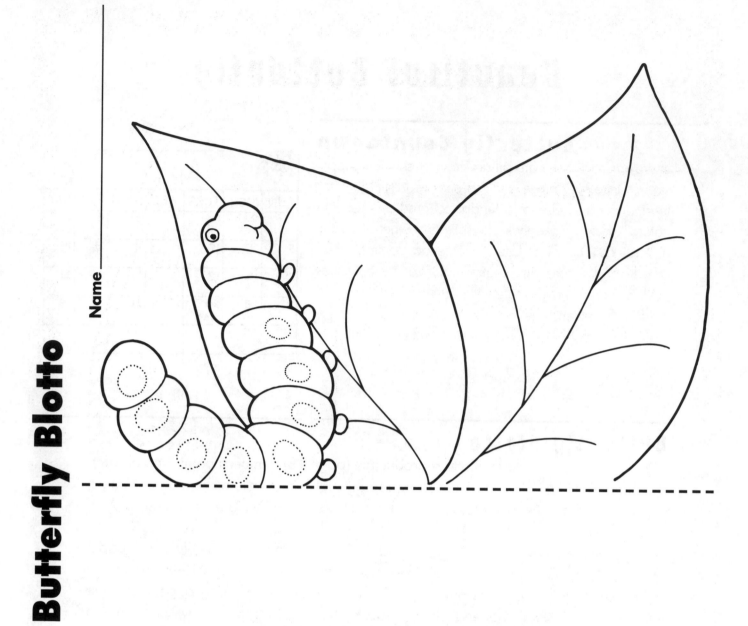

Book Cooks © 2002 Creative Teaching Press

Cowboy Cookies

A Campfire for Cowboy Billy
by Wendy K. Ulmer (Northland Publishing)

Join Cowboy Billy as he rides his stick horse on an imaginary journey through the wild west in memory of his late grandpa. Children will be eager to put on their cowboy boots and join Cowboy Billy as he outsmarts a gang of bandits.

All of your "cowboys" and "cowgirls" will learn about building a "campfire" and making "cowboy" compound words. They will enjoy "roundin' up" some crunchy cowboy cookies for their hearty appetites.

Activity
Cowboy Compounds

Activity
Build a Campfire

Song
"Haystacks"

Cooking Experience
Cowboy Cookies

Related Literature

The Cowboy and the Black-Eyed Pea by Tony Johnston (Paper Star)
Cowboy Cal by Jim Kraft (Troll Communications)
Once There Was a Bull . . . (Frog) by Rick Walton (Gibbs Smith)
White Dynamite and Curly Kidd by Bill Martin Jr. and John Archambault (Henry Holt and Company)

Cowboy Cookies

Math Skill
• measuring

I think this recipe is [ ]

Recipe

Ingredients
• 1 tablespoon peanut butter
• 1 tablespoon dry milk
• 1 teaspoon honey
• 1 tablespoon chow mein noodles

Utensils and Supplies
• measuring spoons
• large plastic cup
• mixing spoon
• waxed paper

Mix together 1 tablespoon peanut butter and 1 tablespoon dry milk in a large plastic cup. Add 1 teaspoon honey and 1 tablespoon chow mein noodles. Spoon the cookie onto a piece of waxed paper.

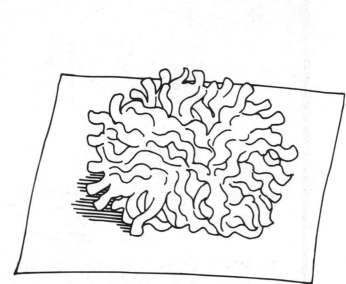

Haystacks
(to the tune of "Twinkle, Twinkle Little Star")

Cowboy cookies,
all crunchy and sweet . . .
They look like haystacks,
but they're a swell treat.

Cowboy Cookies Recipe Cards

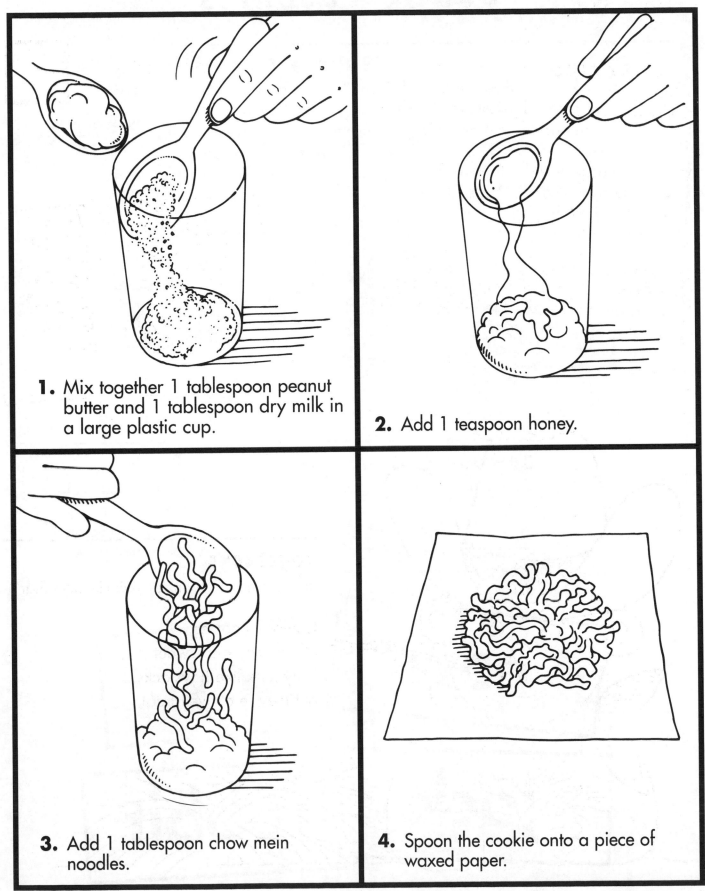

1. Mix together 1 tablespoon peanut butter and 1 tablespoon dry milk in a large plastic cup.

2. Add 1 teaspoon honey.

3. Add 1 tablespoon chow mein noodles.

4. Spoon the cookie onto a piece of waxed paper.

Cowboy Cookies

Build a Campfire

Use **tape** to attach **white twinkling lights** to a 2' (61 cm) cardboard square. Place some **short branches** over the lights, and cover the cardboard, lights, and branches with **red and orange cellophane.** Tape the sides of the cellophane under the cardboard to make a "campfire." Plug the lights into an electric socket or **extension cord.** Turn out the classroom lights, turn on the twinkling lights, and invite children to sit around the campfire and tell stories.

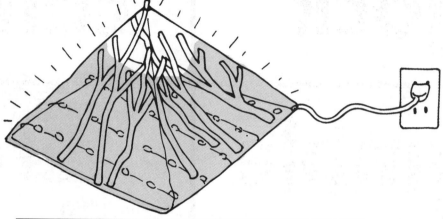

Cowboy Compounds

Copy and cut apart a set of **Cowboy Compound Word Cards (page 23)** for each child. Have children match two words that make a compound word when placed together. Give each child a piece of **construction paper,** and have children glue their compound words on the paper. To extend the activity, invite children to illustrate their words.

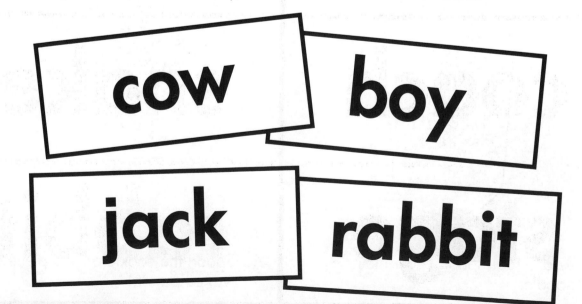

Cowboy Compound Word Cards

cow	boy
jack	camp
tumble	fire
weed	rattle
coach	snake
stage	rabbit

Dandy Dirt Dessert

Worms Wiggle
by David Pelham (Simon & Schuster)

If worms wiggle, what do dogs, snakes, and kittens do? The answers to these questions and many others are found in this exciting pop-up book that uses rhyme to explain how animals move from place to place. Children will be eager to guess the movements of the animals that pop up on the pages.

Children will "squiggle" and "wiggle" in delight as they make worm paintings, explore worms in the dirt, and eat candy worms that jiggle in their mouth.

Activity
Worm Painting

Activity
Dig in the Dirt

Song
"Worm in the Dirt"

Cooking Experience
Dandy Dirt Dessert

Related Literature

Wonderful Worms by Linda Glaser (The Millbrook Press)
Wormology by Michael Elsohn Ross (Carolrhoda Books)
Worms by Theresa Greenaway (Econo-Clad Books))

Dandy Dirt Dessert

Math Skill
- measuring

Name _____

I think this recipe is ☐

Recipe

Ingredients
- 2 tablespoons instant chocolate pudding mix
- 3 tablespoons milk
- 1 chocolate sandwich cookie
- 1 gummy worm

Utensils and Supplies
- measuring spoons
- clear plastic cup
- resealable plastic bag
- plastic spoon

Scoop 2 tablespoons instant chocolate pudding mix into a clear plastic cup. Add 3 tablespoons milk, and stir. While the pudding sets, place a chocolate sandwich cookie in a resealable plastic bag. Seal the bag. Smash the cookie with your fist. Pour the crumbs on top of the pudding. Add a gummy worm.

Worm in the Dirt
(to the tune of "The Farmer in the Dell")

The dandy dirt dessert
Looks all muddy and brown.
Is that a wiggly worm I see?
I'm getting out of town!

Book Cooks © 2002 Creative Teaching Press

Dandy Dirt Dessert Recipe Cards

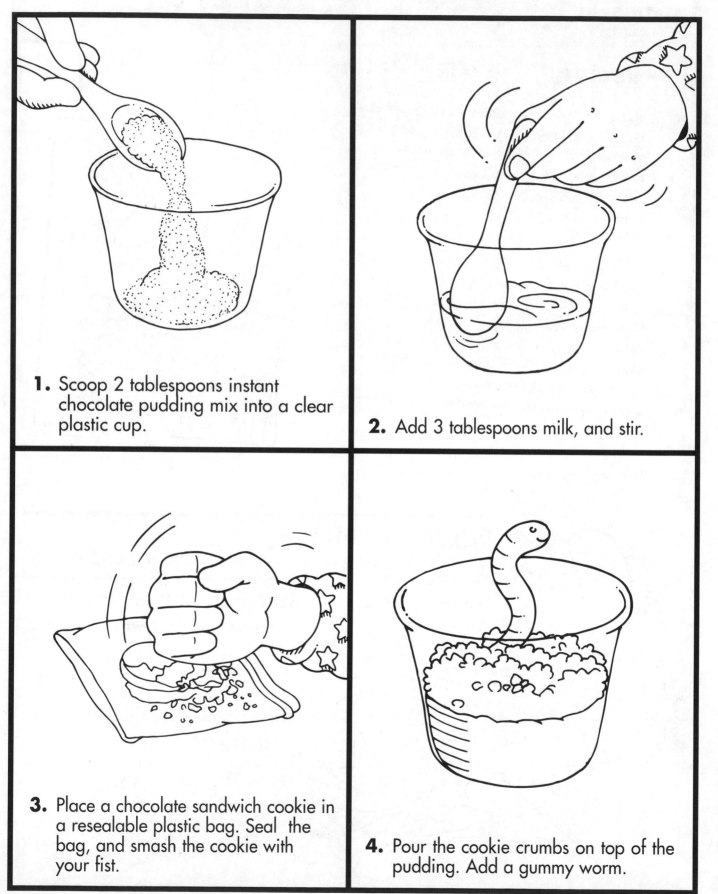

1. Scoop 2 tablespoons instant chocolate pudding mix into a clear plastic cup.

2. Add 3 tablespoons milk, and stir.

3. Place a chocolate sandwich cookie in a resealable plastic bag. Seal the bag, and smash the cookie with your fist.

4. Pour the cookie crumbs on top of the pudding. Add a gummy worm.

Dandy Dirt Dessert

Worm Painting

In advance, purchase **night crawlers** from a sporting goods store. Keep them in the **refrigerator** until you are ready to use them. Rinse them in a **colander.** Put **1 tablespoon water** and **2 drops of food coloring** in a **shallow dish.** Repeat with different colors of food coloring. Place the night crawlers in the dishes until they are covered in food coloring. This is not harmful to the night crawlers. Then, slip them out of the dishes by drawing them to the side, up the side, and over the edge. If you pinch them with your fingers, you will harm them. Give each child a night crawler and a **piece of white paper.** Tell children to carefully place their night crawler on the paper and watch it move around the paper. Have them repeat the activity with different-colored worms. After the activity, put the night crawlers outside in the dirt. Have children write a word or sentence on their paper that describes what the worm "squiggles" look like.

The squiggles are colorful.

Dig in the Dirt

Take children on a walking field trip to explore different types of dirt. Have each child use a **craft stick** to dig in the dirt. Provide **magnifying glasses** for further exploration. Ask children *What do you see?* When you return to the classroom, invite children to write about the things they observed in the dirt.

Egg Salad Crackers

Green Eggs and Ham
by Dr. Seuss (Random House)

In this rhyming book, green eggs and ham are not something Sam likes until he tastes them. He discovers that indeed he does like green eggs and ham. Children will relate to Sam and his fear of trying new foods.

Even Sam-I-Am would enjoy some delicious egg salad crackers. Children will learn about what eggs are "cracked up" to be by graphing and estimating information about eggs and then preparing an "eggcellent" recipe.

Activity
How Do You Like Your Eggs?

Activity
A Jar of Eggs

Song
"Egg Salad Crackers Yum Yum"

Cooking Experience
Egg Salad Crackers

Related Literature

Bently and Egg by William Joyce (HarperCollins)
An Extraordinary Egg by Leo Lionni (Alfred A. Knopf Books)
Rechenka's Eggs by Patricia Polacco (Putnam)

Egg Salad Crackers

Math Skill
• measuring

I think this recipe is ☐

Recipe

Ingredients
• 1 hard-boiled egg
• salt
• 2 tablespoons mayonnaise
• 4 crackers

Utensils and Supplies
• plastic cup
• plastic fork
• measuring spoon
• plastic knife
• paper plate

Peel one hard-boiled egg. Crumble it in a cup with a fork. Add a dash of salt and 2 table-spoons mayonnaise. Mix well. Spread the egg salad on crackers.

Egg Salad Crackers Yum Yum
(to the tune of "Davy Crockett")

Egg salad crackers,
Oh, yummy, yum, yum.
Peel the egg, then mush it.
You are sure to have some fun.

Add a dash of salt
And a dab of mayonnaise.
Spread it on a cracker,
And you will be amazed.

Egg Salad Crackers Recipe Cards

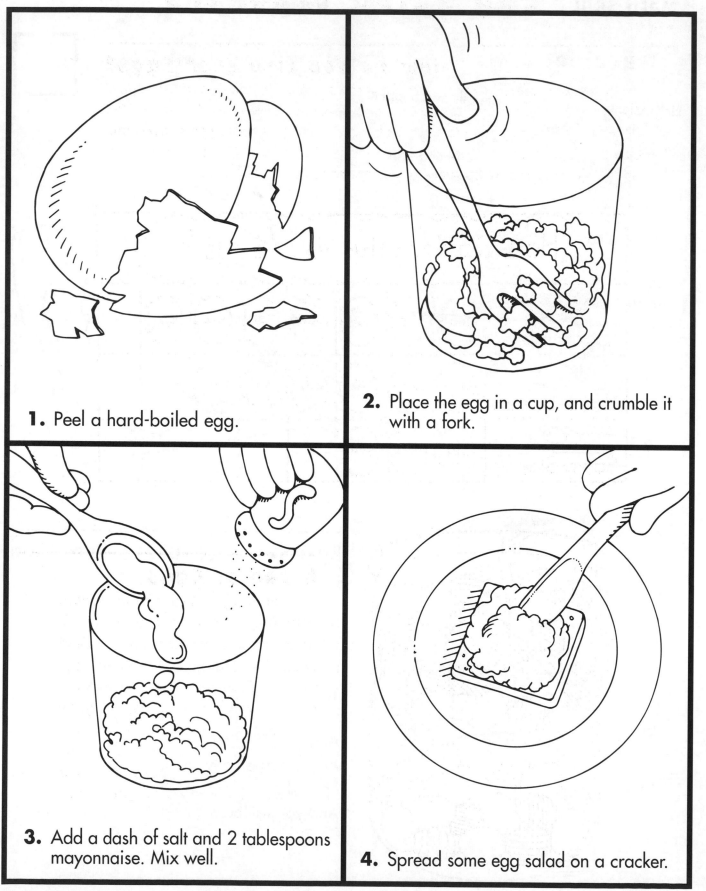

1. Peel a hard-boiled egg.

2. Place the egg in a cup, and crumble it with a fork.

3. Add a dash of salt and 2 tablespoons mayonnaise. Mix well.

4. Spread some egg salad on a cracker.

Egg Salad Crackers

How Do You Like Your Eggs?

Draw on **chart paper** a graph with three rows. Label the rows *Scrambled, Hard-Boiled,* and *Sunny-Side Up,* and draw corresponding pictures. Title the graph *How Do You Like Your Eggs?* Write each child's name on a separate **egg-shaped die-cut,** and place **tape** on the back of the die-cuts. Ask children to place their die-cut on the graph to show their favorite way to eat eggs.

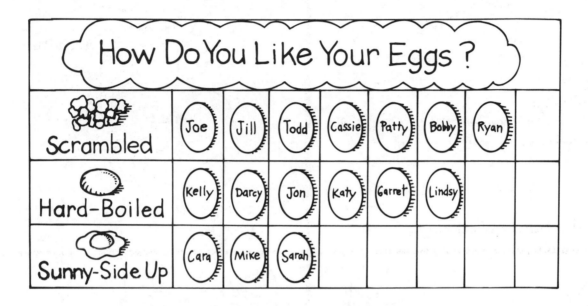

How Do You Like Your Eggs?								
Scrambled	Joe	Jill	Todd	Cassie	Patty	Bobby	Ryan	
Hard-Boiled	Kelly	Darcy	Jon	Katy	Garret	Lindsy		
Sunny-Side Up	Cara	Mike	Sarah					

A Jar of Eggs

Fill a **jar** with **jelly beans** ("eggs"). Have children estimate the number of eggs in the jar. Record their estimations on **chart paper.** Invite the class to count the eggs together. Give each child a handful of eggs. Have children sort their eggs by color and then count the number of eggs in each color. To extend the activity, give each child a piece of paper, and have children use the eggs to create math equations.

Fabulous Flower

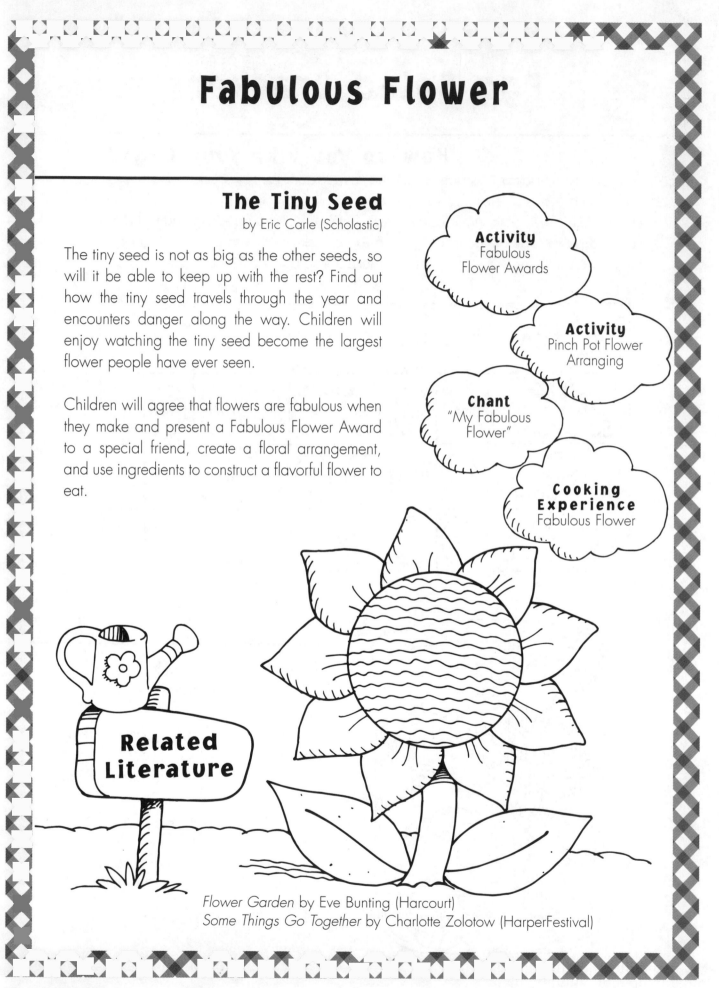

The Tiny Seed
by Eric Carle (Scholastic)

The tiny seed is not as big as the other seeds, so will it be able to keep up with the rest? Find out how the tiny seed travels through the year and encounters danger along the way. Children will enjoy watching the tiny seed become the largest flower people have ever seen.

Children will agree that flowers are fabulous when they make and present a Fabulous Flower Award to a special friend, create a floral arrangement, and use ingredients to construct a flavorful flower to eat.

Activity
Fabulous Flower Awards

Activity
Pinch Pot Flower Arranging

Chant
"My Fabulous Flower"

Cooking Experience
Fabulous Flower

Related Literature

Flower Garden by Eve Bunting (Harcourt)
Some Things Go Together by Charlotte Zolotow (HarperFestival)

Fabulous Flower

Math Skill
- sequencing

I think this recipe is

Recipe

Ingredients
- green gelatin
- red gelatin
- 1 sour green licorice whip
- 1 large gumdrop

Utensils and Supplies
- heart-shaped cookie cutters
- paper plate

In advance, make green and red gelatin, and chill it in the refrigerator. Use a cookie cutter to cut two green hearts and three red hearts from the gelatin. Place one licorice whip on a plate to make the "stem." Add two green hearts to the sides of the licorice to make "leaves." Place the tips of three red hearts at the top of the licorice to make "petals." Squish a gumdrop in between the red hearts. Then, enjoy eating your yummy "flower."

My Fabulous Flower
(chant rhythmically)

Squiggle your licorice across the paper plate.
Add two leaves that are green.
Three red hearts a fabulous flower makes.
Now squish a gooey gumdrop in between.

Fabulous Flower Recipe Cards

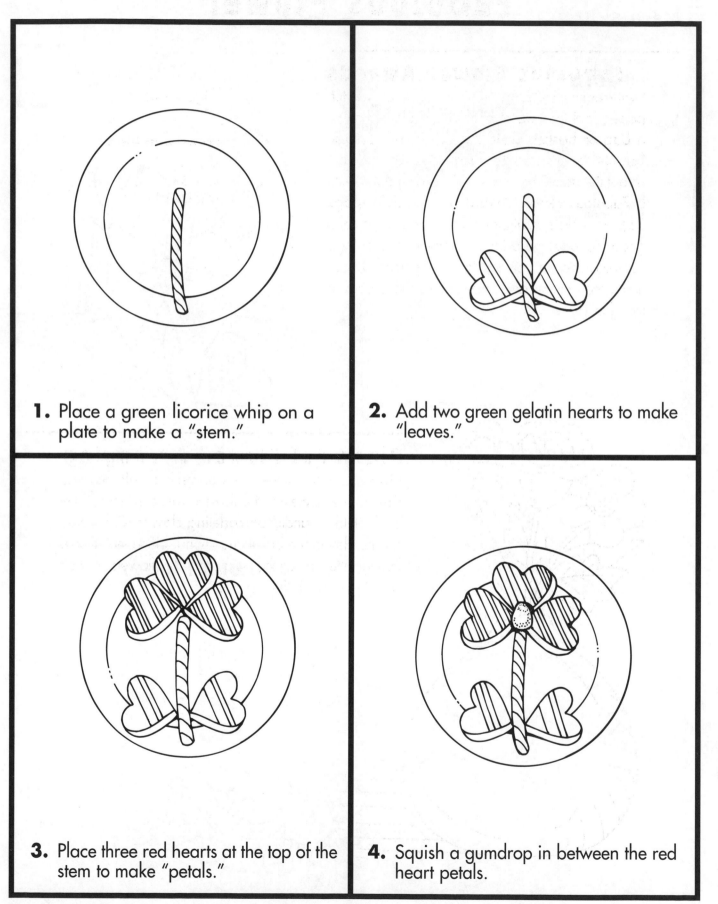

1. Place a green licorice whip on a plate to make a "stem."

2. Add two green gelatin hearts to make "leaves."

3. Place three red hearts at the top of the stem to make "petals."

4. Squish a gumdrop in between the red heart petals.

Fabulous Flower

Fabulous Flower Awards

Write each child's name on a piece of **scratch paper,** fold the papers in half, and place them in a **bag or basket.** Have each child pick a name from the bag or basket, and ask children not to reveal the name they chose. Then, give each child a **Fabulous Flower Award reproducible (page 36).** As a class, brainstorm the characteristics of a good friend. Have children complete and color a Fabulous Flower Award for the person whose name they chose and then present the award to their friend.

Pinch Pot Flower Arranging

Give each child three types of **fresh or silk flowers.** Discuss the names of the flowers with the class. Give each child a handful of **modeling clay.** Have children roll the clay into a ball in their hand, place their thumb through the top of their clay, put the flowers in their "pot," and pinch the top closed.

Fabulous Flower Award

Presented to: _____

From: _____

For: _____

_____

Granny's Granola

Our Granny
by Margaret Wild (Houghton Mifflin)

Grannies come in all shapes and sizes, live in different places, have different hairstyles, work at different jobs, drive different automobiles, and give different types of kisses. But, as two children discuss the differences in grannies, they realize their own granny is the perfect granny to have.

Grannies are great and so is their granola. Children will learn to sort objects by common attributes, count by tens, and write a friendly letter to Granny. Children will enjoy shaking up and then eating up their great granola treat.

Activity
Count by 10s

Activity
Thank You, Granny

Song
"Granny's Glorious Treat"

Cooking Experience
Granny's Granola

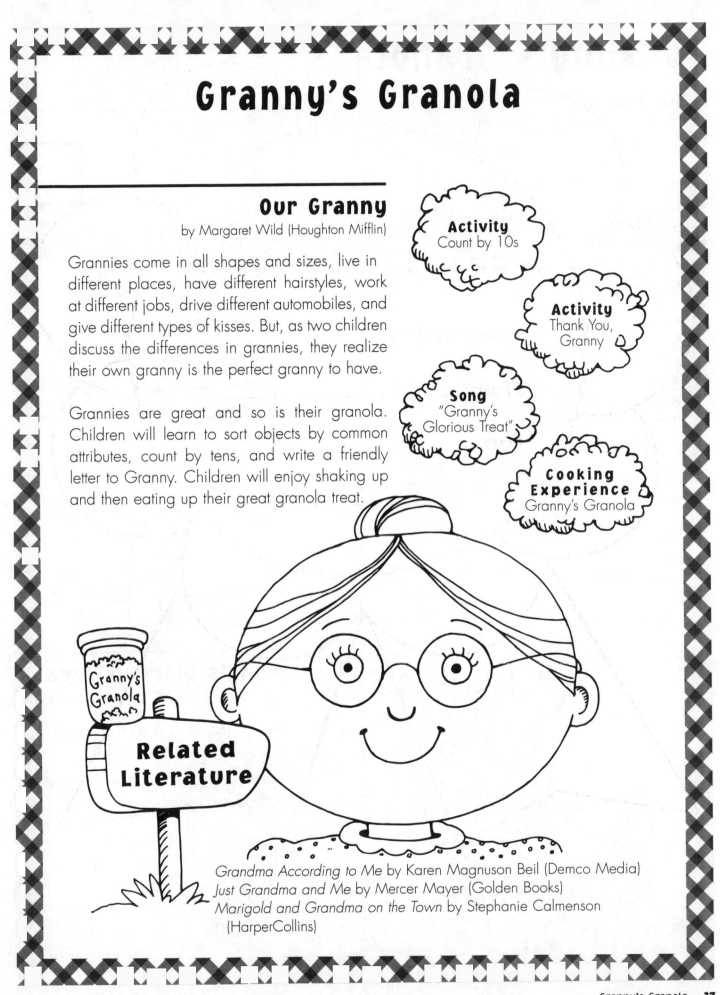

Related Literature

Grandma According to Me by Karen Magnuson Beil (Demco Media)
Just Grandma and Me by Mercer Mayer (Golden Books)
Marigold and Grandma on the Town by Stephanie Calmenson (HarperCollins)

Granny's Granola

Math Skills
- counting by 10s
- sorting

I think this recipe is ☐

Recipe

Ingredients
- O-shaped cereal
- raisins
- unshelled sunflower seeds
- pretzels
- banana chips
- almonds
- chocolate chips
- dried pineapple cubes
- mini-marshmallows
- M&M's®

Utensils and Supplies
- crayons or markers
- small paper bag

Decorate a small paper bag. Place ten of each ingredient in ten piles. Count the ingredients by tens. Place the piles in the bag. Fold over the top of the bag, and shake it to make a yummy treat!

Granny's Glorious Treat
(to the tune of "The Farmer in the Dell")

Granny's granola's a glorious treat.
It's goofy. It's grand. It's great.
It makes you giggle. It makes you glad.
It really is first-rate.

Book Cooks © 2002 Creative Teaching Press

Granny's Granola Recipe Cards

1. Place ten of each ingredient in ten piles.

2. Place the piles in the bag.

3. Fold over the top of the bag.

4. Shake!

Granny's Granola

Count by 10s

Give each child ten sets of ten **small manipulatives (e.g., cereal, paper clips)** and a **Granny's Granola Counting Mat (page 41).** Invite children to sort the manipulatives by common attributes and place them in ten piles on their counting mat. Have them draw or glue on their paper each group of manipulatives and then count the groups. Ask children to name the manipulatives and explain their counting method.

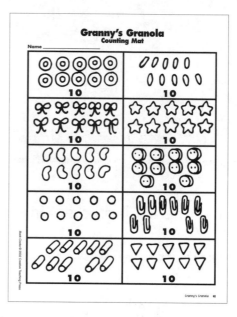

Thank You, Granny

Brainstorm with the class attributes that make a grandmother special. For example, a grandmother gives great hugs, or she always has a big smile. Give each child a piece of paper. Have them write a letter thanking Granny for the granola and explaining to Granny why they think she is a special person. Encourage children to draw a picture for Granny. To extend the activity, give each child an envelope. Explain how to address an envelope. Invite children to address their envelope and draw a postage stamp.

Granny's Granola
Counting Mat

Name _____

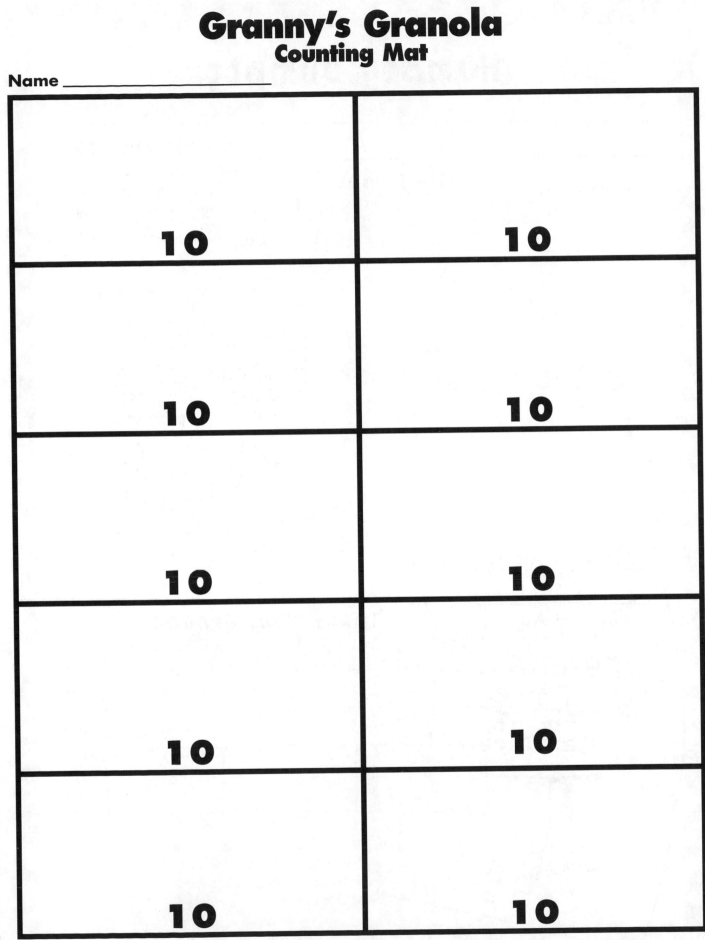

Humpty Dumpty

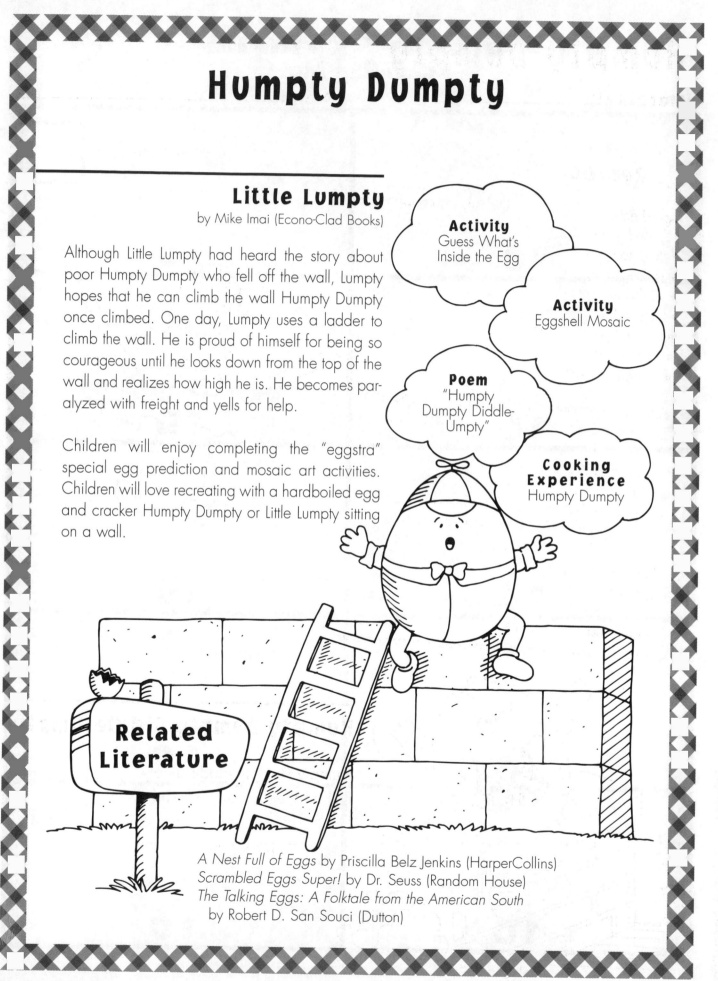

Little Lumpty

by Mike Imai (Econo-Clad Books)

Although Little Lumpty had heard the story about poor Humpty Dumpty who fell off the wall, Lumpty hopes that he can climb the wall Humpty Dumpty once climbed. One day, Lumpty uses a ladder to climb the wall. He is proud of himself for being so courageous until he looks down from the top of the wall and realizes how high he is. He becomes paralyzed with freight and yells for help.

Children will enjoy completing the "eggstra" special egg prediction and mosaic art activities. Children will love recreating with a hardboiled egg and cracker Humpty Dumpty or Little Lumpty sitting on a wall.

Activity
Guess What's Inside the Egg

Activity
Eggshell Mosaic

Poem
"Humpty Dumpty Diddle-Umpty"

Cooking Experience
Humpty Dumpty

Related Literature

A Nest Full of Eggs by Priscilla Belz Jenkins (HarperCollins)
Scrambled Eggs Super! by Dr. Seuss (Random House)
The Talking Eggs: A Folktale from the American South
   by Robert D. San Souci (Dutton)

Humpty Dumpty

Math Skill
• identifying shapes

I think this recipe is ☐

Recipe

Ingredients
• $\frac{1}{2}$ hard-boiled egg
• 1 rectangular cracker
• mayonnaise
• O-shaped cereal
• mustard
• 2 small pretzel sticks
• 2 celery stalks
• 1 Gummy Bear®

Utensils and Supplies
• plastic knife
• paper plate

Place a rectangular cracker flat on a paper plate. Set half of a hard-boiled egg (yolk side facing down) on the top edge of the cracker. Frost the backs of O-shaped cereal with mayonnaise, and place the cereal on the egg to make "eyes" and a "mouth." Add a little mustard and mayonnaise on the egg to make "hair." Add mustard to two pretzel sticks and two celery sticks, and attach them to the cracker to make "arms" and "legs." Spread a little mayonnaise on the back of a Gummy Bear®, and place it horizontally on the egg to make a bow tie.

Humpty Dumpty Diddle-Umpty

Humpty Dumpty diddle-umpty
Fell off the wall on his head.
His mother and father and all the king's men
Took him quickly home to bed.

Humpty Dumpty Recipe Cards

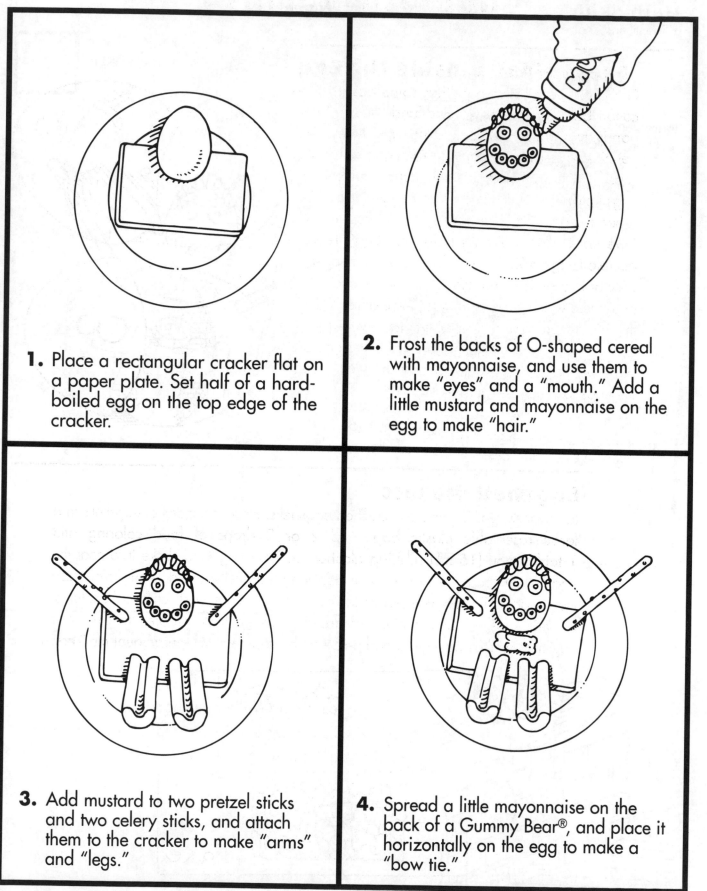

1. Place a rectangular cracker flat on a paper plate. Set half of a hard-boiled egg on the top edge of the cracker.

2. Frost the backs of O-shaped cereal with mayonnaise, and use them to make "eyes" and a "mouth." Add a little mustard and mayonnaise on the egg to make "hair."

3. Add mustard to two pretzel sticks and two celery sticks, and attach them to the cracker to make "arms" and "legs."

4. Spread a little mayonnaise on the back of a Gummy Bear®, and place it horizontally on the egg to make a "bow tie."

Humpty Dumpty

Guess What's Inside the Egg

Gather twelve **plastic eggs (that come apart)**, one **cotton ball**, one **piece of hard candy**, two **rubber bands**, two **Unifix® cubes**, one **eraser**, one **key**, two **pennies**, one **small bell**, one **marble**, three **paper clips**, two **hairpins**, and two **buttons**. Number the eggs from 1 to 12. Place each of the listed items in a separate egg, and store the eggs in an egg carton. Give each child a **What's Inside the Egg? reproducible (page 46)**. Invite children to work independently or in a small group. Have them shake each egg and guess which items are inside. Tell children to find the picture on their reproducible that matches their guess. Have them write the number of the egg on their paper. At the end of the activity, invite children to open the eggs to check their answers.

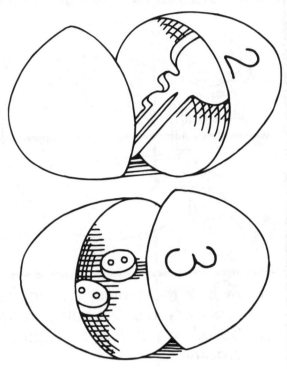

Eggshell Mosaic

In advance, gather numerous **crushed eggshells**. Place a handful of eggshells in a **large resealable plastic bag**. Add **2 or 3 drops of food coloring** and **1 tablespoon (15 mL) rubbing alcohol**. Seal the bag, and shake it to coat the eggshells. Repeat this process with additional eggshells and different colors. Lay the eggshells flat on **newspaper** to dry overnight. Give each child a handful of colored eggshells and a piece of **drawing paper**. Invite children to glue their eggshells on their paper and add details to the eggshells with **permanent markers**.

What's Inside the Egg?

Name _____

Item	Egg Number	Item	Egg Number
cotton ball		pennies	
candy		bell	
rubber bands		marble	
Unifix® Cubes		paper clips	
eraser		hairpins	
key		buttons	

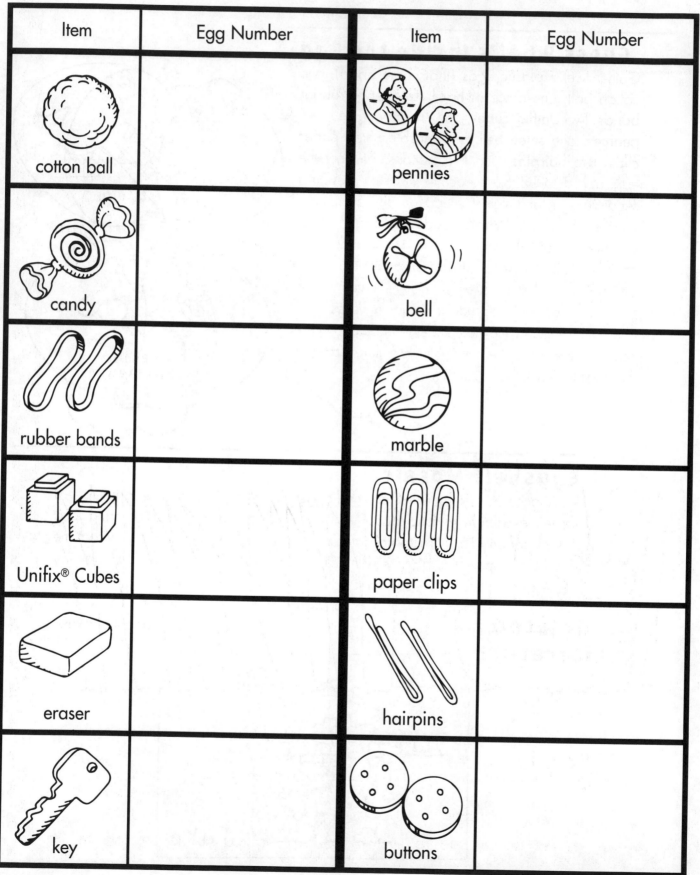

Ichabod the Inchworm

Inch by Inch
by Leo Lionni (Mulberry Books)

A charming inchworm boasts about his abilities to measure anything under the sun. He is tested by a nightingale who challenges the inchworm to measure the nightingale's song.

Children will boast about their ability to learn measuring skills, feel self-assured when they learn some new *i* words, and enjoy the sweet inchworm treat.

Activity
Ichabod the Inchworm

Activity
Inchworm "I" Words

Song
"Ichabod"

Cooking Experience
Ichabod the Inchworm

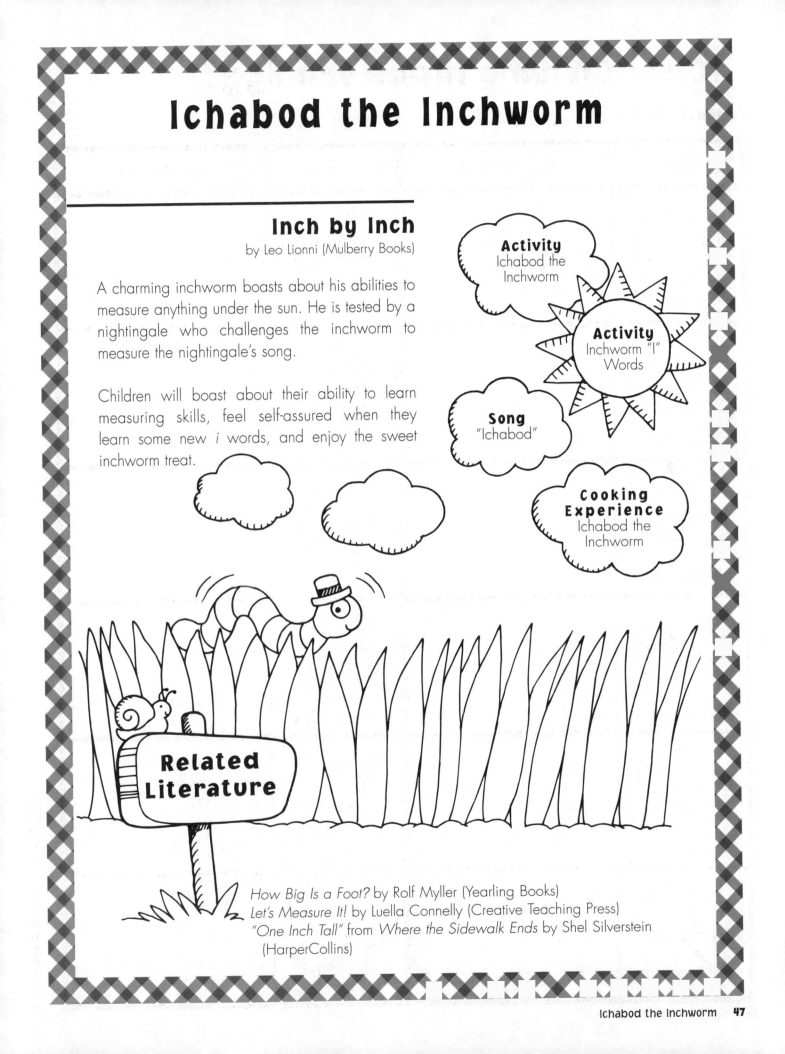

Related Literature

How Big Is a Foot? by Rolf Myller (Yearling Books)
Let's Measure It! by Luella Connelly (Creative Teaching Press)
"One Inch Tall" from *Where the Sidewalk Ends* by Shel Silverstein (HarperCollins)

Ichabod the Inchworm

Math Skill
- measuring

Name _____

I think this recipe is ☐

Recipe

Ingredients
- 1 bread stick (plain)
- green icing or softened cream cheese
- black or red licorice ropes
- small candies

Utensils and Supplies
- plastic knife
- paper plate

Frost a 12" (30.5 cm) or longer bread stick with green icing or softened cream cheese. Use 1" (2.5 cm) segments of black or red licorice ropes to mark inches (centimeters) on the "inchworm's" back. Add small candies to make "eyes."

Ichabod
(to the tune of "A Tisket, A Tasket")

Ichabod the inchworm
Does nothing but measure each day.
If you don't want him crawling all over you,
You'd better stay out of his way.

Ichabod the Inchworm Recipe Cards

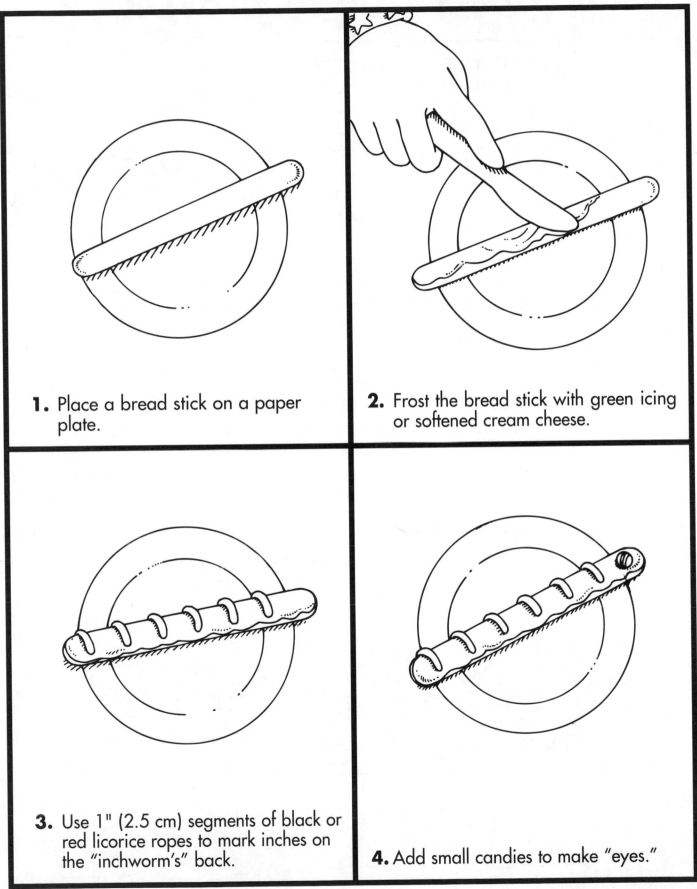

1. Place a bread stick on a paper plate.

2. Frost the bread stick with green icing or softened cream cheese.

3. Use 1" (2.5 cm) segments of black or red licorice ropes to mark inches on the "inchworm's" back.

4. Add small candies to make "eyes."

Ichabod the Inchworm

Ichabod the Inchworm

Give each child an **Ichabod the Inchworm repro-ducible (page 51).** Invite children to color and cut out their ruler. Explain how to use the ruler to measure objects, and demonstrate by measuring several classroom objects. Invite children to work with a partner to measure various classroom objects. Walk around the classroom, and help children use their ruler. When they are finished, ask them questions such as *Which object that you measured is six inches? How many inches is the smallest object you measured?*

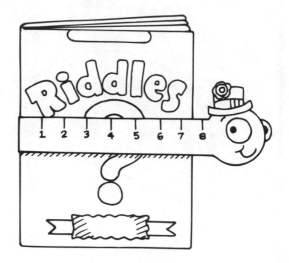

Inchworm "I" Words

Give each child an **Inchworm "I" Words reproducible (page 52).** Divide the class into pairs. Give each pair a **dictionary,** and ask pairs to find five words that begin with the letter *i*. Have children write each word in a separate circle on their reproducible and then illustrate the words. Invite each child to cut out the circles and glue them to a **long strip of construction paper** to make an "inchworm." Display the completed worms on a bulletin board. Invite children to read the worms.

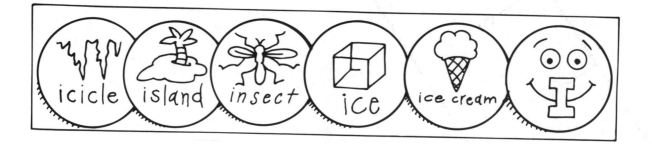

Ichabod the Inchworm

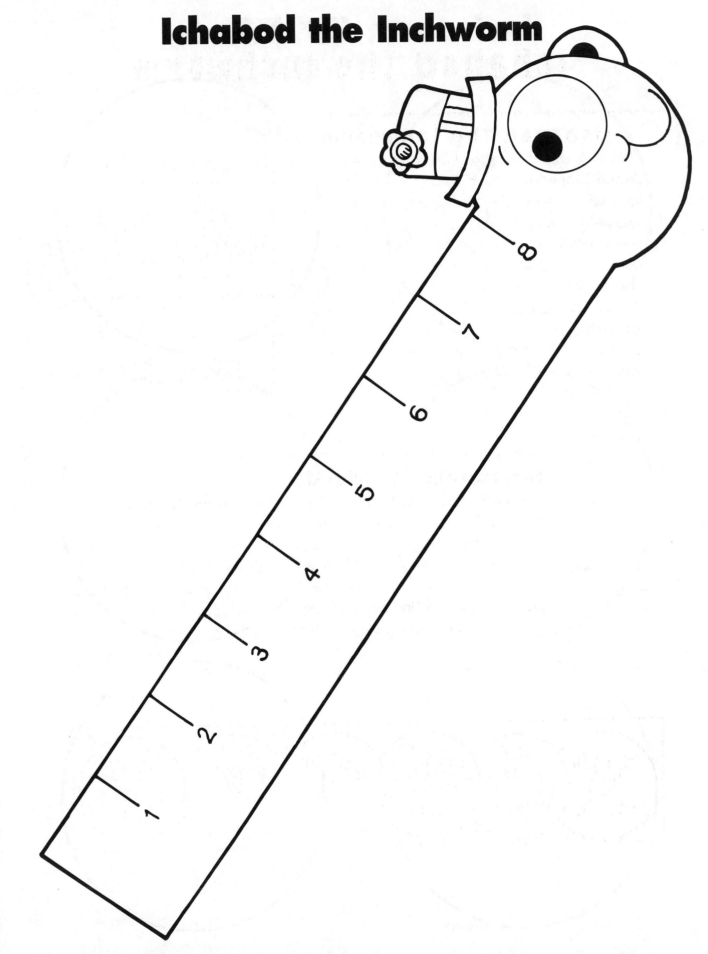

Inchworm "I" Words

Jolly Jack-O

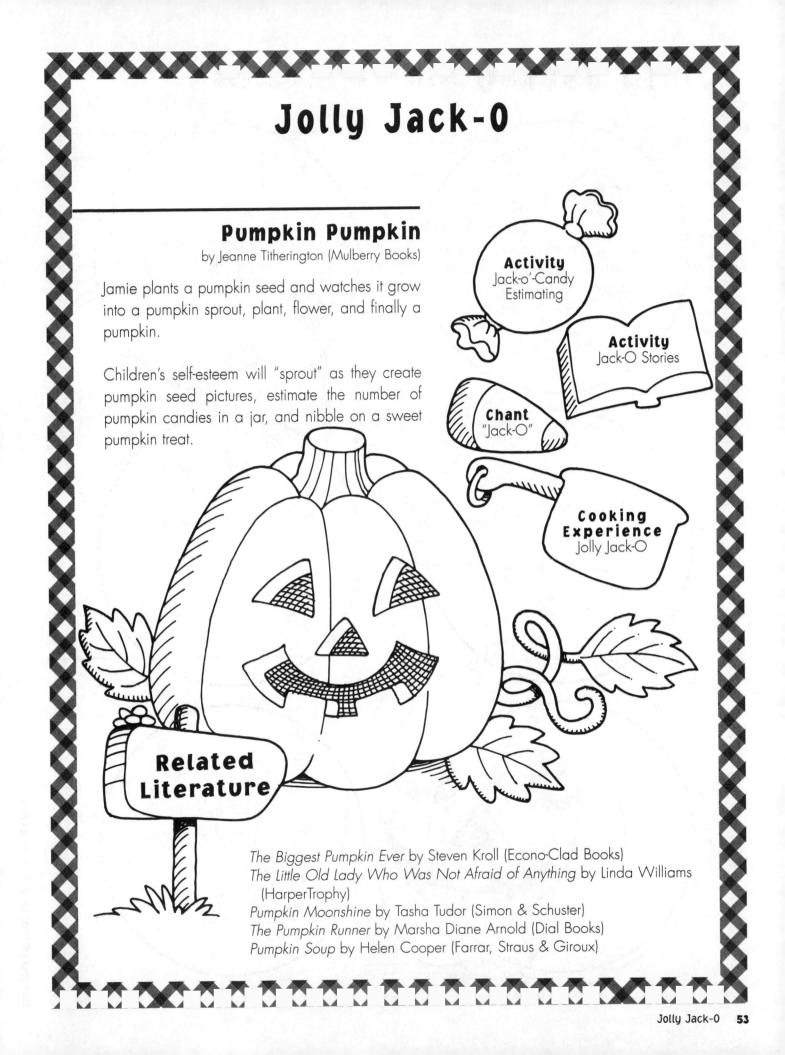

Pumpkin Pumpkin
by Jeanne Titherington (Mulberry Books)

Jamie plants a pumpkin seed and watches it grow into a pumpkin sprout, plant, flower, and finally a pumpkin.

Children's self-esteem will "sprout" as they create pumpkin seed pictures, estimate the number of pumpkin candies in a jar, and nibble on a sweet pumpkin treat.

Activity
Jack-o'-Candy Estimating

Activity
Jack-O Stories

Chant
"Jack-O"

Cooking Experience
Jolly Jack-O

Related Literature

The Biggest Pumpkin Ever by Steven Kroll (Econo-Clad Books)
The Little Old Lady Who Was Not Afraid of Anything by Linda Williams (HarperTrophy)
Pumpkin Moonshine by Tasha Tudor (Simon & Schuster)
The Pumpkin Runner by Marsha Diane Arnold (Dial Books)
Pumpkin Soup by Helen Cooper (Farrar, Straus & Giroux)

Jolly Jack-O

Math Skill
- patterning

I think this recipe is ▢

Recipe

Ingredients
- 16 ounces softened cream cheese
- orange food coloring
- 1 piece of bread
- raisins
- chocolate chips
- candy corn
- paper plate

Utensils and Supplies
- bowl
- mixing spoon
- pumpkin cookie cutter (optional)
- plastic knife
- paper plate

Mix in a bowl 16 ounces softened cream cheese with orange food coloring. Use a pumpkin cookie cutter or plastic knife to cut a pumpkin shape from a piece of bread. Spread the cream cheese on the bread. Use raisins, chocolate chips, and candy corn to make a pattern on the pumpkin.

Jack-O
(chant rhythmically)

Jolly Jack-O
Has a great big smile,
And his face is covered with cheese.
He winks his eye and happily says,
"Take a bite, if you please."

Jolly Jack-O Recipe Cards

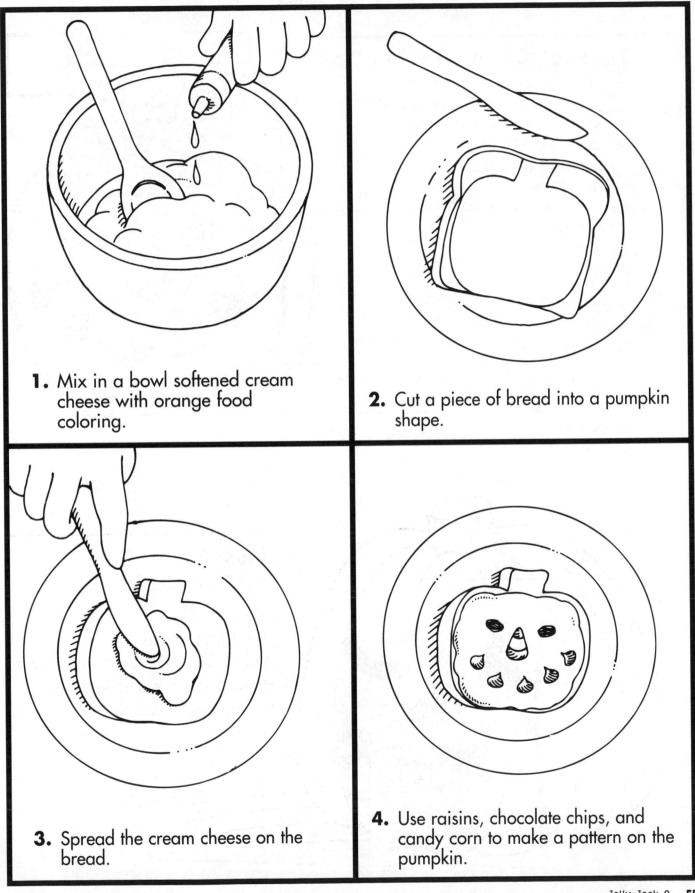

1. Mix in a bowl softened cream cheese with orange food coloring.

2. Cut a piece of bread into a pumpkin shape.

3. Spread the cream cheese on the bread.

4. Use raisins, chocolate chips, and candy corn to make a pattern on the pumpkin.

Jolly Jack-O

Jack-o'-Candy Estimating

Fill a **jar** with **pumpkin-shaped candies**. Have each child estimate the number of candies in the jar. Record the estimations on **butcher paper**. Invite the class to count the candies together. Give each child a handful of candies from the jar. Encourage children to put them in groups of fives and count the number of groups they have. Count with the class all their candies by fives.

Jack-O Stories

Give each child a handful of clean and dry **pumpkin seeds** and a piece of **drawing paper**. Invite children to glue their seeds onto the paper to make a seed picture. Have each child write a story about his or her picture. Glue the picture and the story to a piece of **construction paper**. Invite children to share their story with the class.

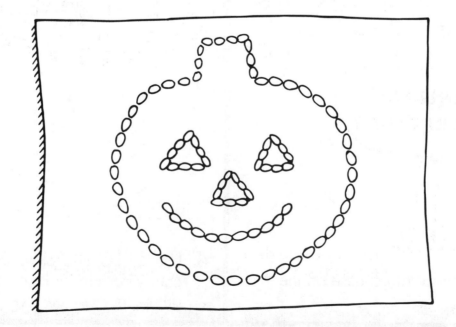

Kabobs of Fruit

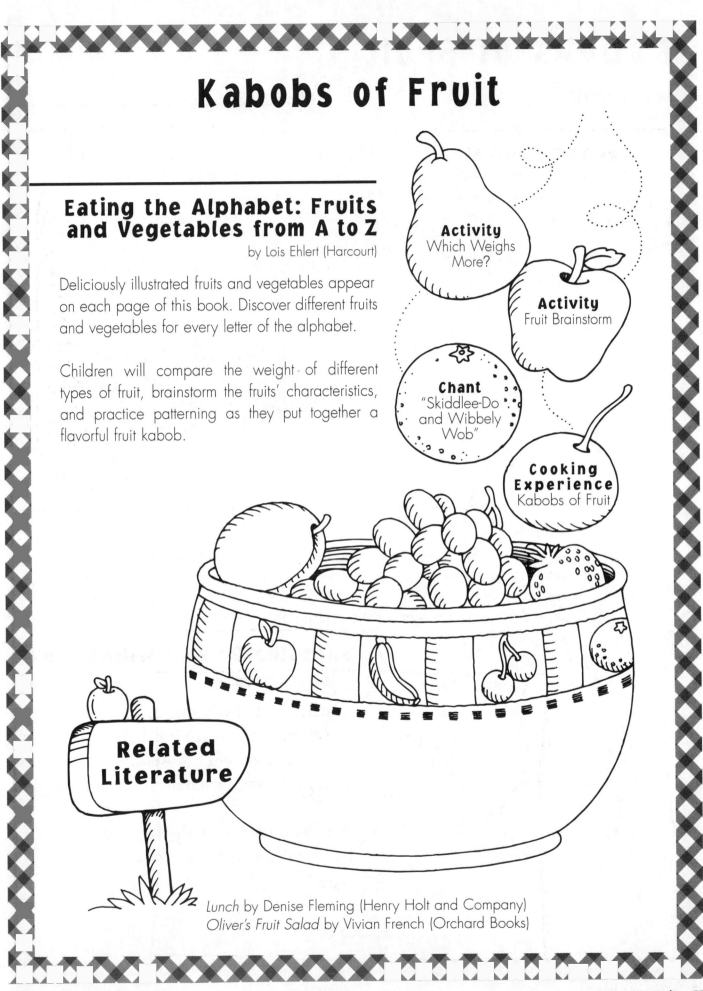

Eating the Alphabet: Fruits and Vegetables from A to Z

by Lois Ehlert (Harcourt)

Deliciously illustrated fruits and vegetables appear on each page of this book. Discover different fruits and vegetables for every letter of the alphabet.

Children will compare the weight of different types of fruit, brainstorm the fruits' characteristics, and practice patterning as they put together a flavorful fruit kabob.

Activity
Which Weighs More?

Activity
Fruit Brainstorm

Chant
"Skiddlee-Do and Wibbely Wob"

Cooking Experience
Kabobs of Fruit

Related Literature

Lunch by Denise Fleming (Henry Holt and Company)
Oliver's Fruit Salad by Vivian French (Orchard Books)

Kabobs of Fruit

Math Skill
• patterning

Name_____

I think this recipe is ☐

Recipe

Ingredients
• variety of fresh fruit
• cinnamon

Utensils and Supplies
• sharp knife
  (adult use only)
• wooden skewer
• paper plate

Ask an adult to wash assorted pieces of fruit and cut them into cubes. Arrange the fruit in a pattern. Slide the fruit onto a wooden skewer. Sprinkle with cinnamon.

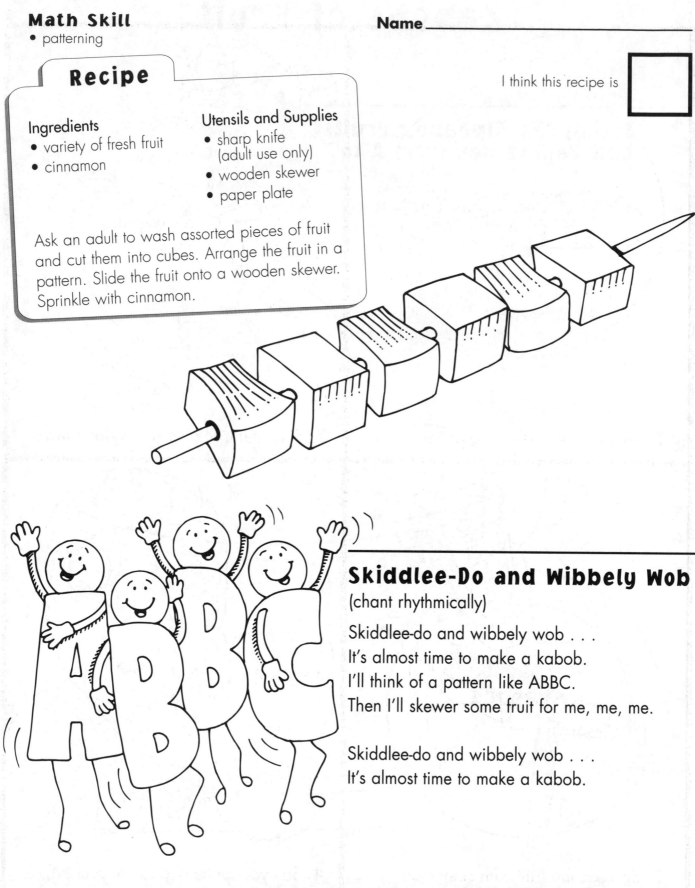

Skiddlee-Do and Wibbely Wob
(chant rhythmically)

Skiddlee-do and wibbely wob . . .
It's almost time to make a kabob.
I'll think of a pattern like ABBC.
Then I'll skewer some fruit for me, me, me.

Skiddlee-do and wibbely wob . . .
It's almost time to make a kabob.

Kabobs of Fruit Recipe Cards

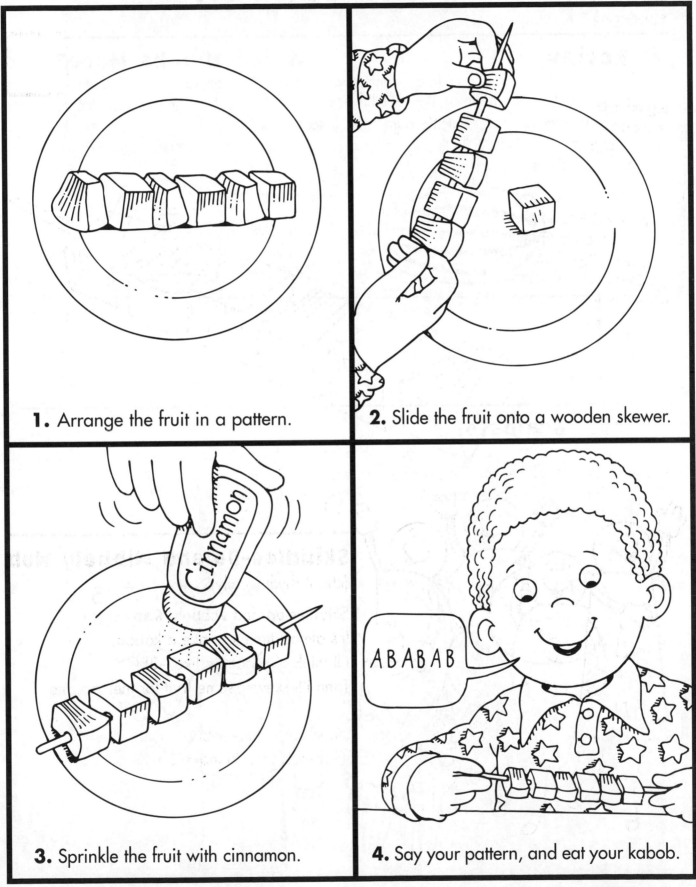

1. Arrange the fruit in a pattern.

2. Slide the fruit onto a wooden skewer.

ABABAB

3. Sprinkle the fruit with cinnamon.

4. Say your pattern, and eat your kabob.

Cinnamon

Kabobs of Fruit

Which Weighs More?

Place different types of **fruit (e.g., cantaloupe, watermelon, apple)** on a table. Have children predict which fruit will weigh the most and which fruit will weigh the least. Record predictions on a piece of **butcher paper.** Use a **scale** to weigh the fruit. Invite volunteers to arrange the fruit in order from greatest to smallest weight. Compare predictions with the actual weight of each fruit.

Fruit Brainstorm

Divide the class into pairs. Give each pair a piece of **fruit.** Have children brainstorm the characteristics of their fruit. For example, a child might say *An apple tastes sour. It is red. It is smooth. The skin has no taste.* Invite each pair to hide their piece of fruit and have the class guess the fruit as they describe it.

Leprechaun Pie

Tim O'Toole and the Wee Folk: An Irish Tale
by Gerald McDermott (Puffin)

Tim O'Toole and his wife were very poor. One day, they had no more food to eat. Tim O'Toole set off to find some work, but he could not find work anywhere. As he was walking, he discovered the hiding place of the wee folk. He knew that the person who spies on the wee folk during the light of day is entitled to their treasure. Tim O'Toole was too trusting, however, and everything given to him by the wee folk was stolen. Fortunately, the wee folk come to his rescue, recover his treasure, and Tim and his wife live happily ever after.

Tim O'Toole and the wee folk will get children in the mood for their own leprechaun fun. Children will go on a treasure hunt, use Lucky Charms® cereal to create a pattern, and make some delicious leprechaun pie.

Activity
Chase a Leprechaun

Activity
Lucky Charm Pattern

Song
"The Clever Leprechaun"

Cooking Experience
Leprechaun Pie

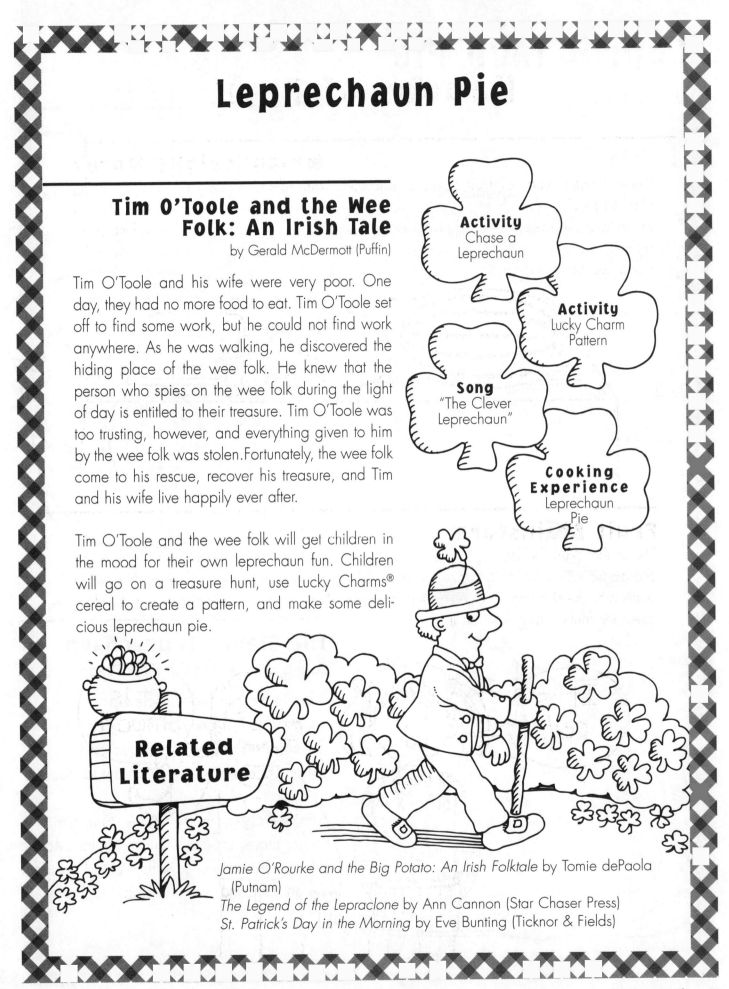

Related Literature

Jamie O'Rourke and the Big Potato: An Irish Folktale by Tomie dePaola (Putnam)
The Legend of the Lepraclone by Ann Cannon (Star Chaser Press)
St. Patrick's Day in the Morning by Eve Bunting (Ticknor & Fields)

Leprechaun Pie

Math Skill
- measuring

Recipe

Ingredients
- 2 tablespoons instant pistachio pudding mix
- 3 tablespoons milk
- 1 foil-wrapped chocolate coin
- whipped cream

Utensils and Supplies
- measuring spoons
- clear plastic cup
- plastic spoon

Scoop 2 tablespoons instant pistachio pudding mix into a clear plastic cup. Add 3 tablespoons milk. Stir. Drop a foil-wrapped chocolate coin into the pudding. Top with whipped cream.

Name _____

I think this recipe is ☐

The Clever Leprechaun
(to the tune of "Up On the Rooftop")

Leprechaun pie hides a clever treat.
It's wrapped in gold, but it's good to eat.
Green and fluffy, with a cloud on top.
When it's gone, we won't want to stop.

Yum, yum, yum in my tummy, tum, tum.
I want more, please Mummy, Mum, Mum.
Oh, green and fluffy, with a cloud on top.
When it's gone, we will stop, stop, stop.

Leprechaun Pie Recipe Cards

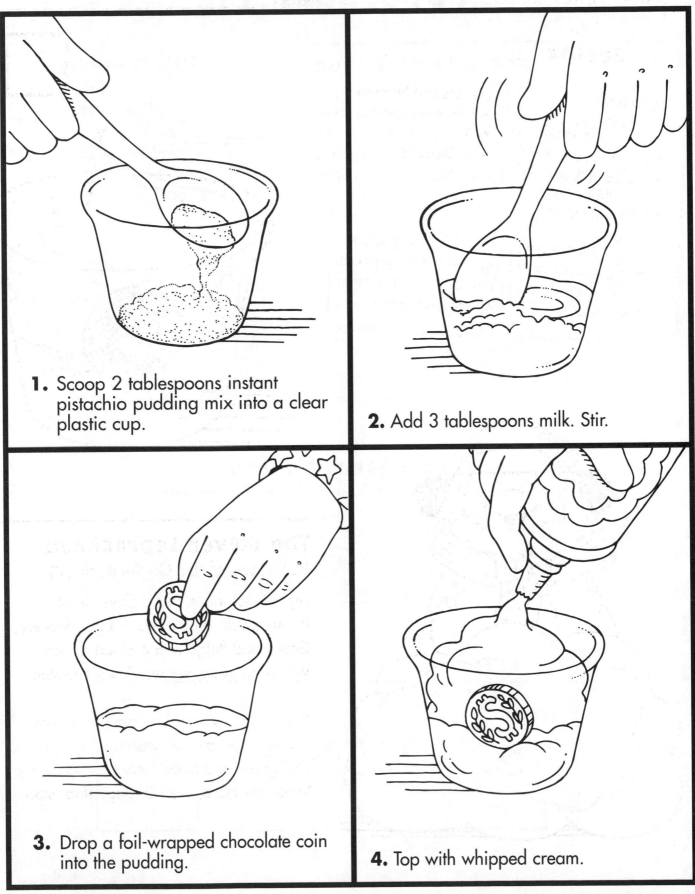

1. Scoop 2 tablespoons instant pistachio pudding mix into a clear plastic cup.

2. Add 3 tablespoons milk. Stir.

3. Drop a foil-wrapped chocolate coin into the pudding.

4. Top with whipped cream.

Leprechaun Pie

Chase a Leprechaun

In advance, make a treasure chest out of an **old shoe box.** Fill it with **treats (e.g., stickers, cookies, pencils).** Hide the treasure chest in or near your classroom. Copy the **Leprechaun Treasure Hunt reproducible (page 65)** on **green paper.** Fill in the blank lines on the shamrocks so that children can determine where the treasure is hidden. Cut out the shamrocks. Place the shamrocks along a predetermined path. Then, invite children to go on the treasure hunt. Read the first clue, and have children carefully walk together to the next shamrock. Repeat with each shamrock until children find the treasure chest. Give each child a treat from the chest.

Lucky Charm Pattern

Give each child a handful of **Lucky Charms® cereal** and a piece of **construction paper.** Invite children to make a pattern with their cereal. Then, invite them to glue their cereal pattern on their paper. Have children share their pattern with the class. To extend the activity, invite children to work with a partner. Have the pairs explain their pattern to the class.

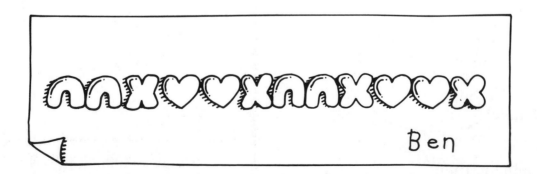

Leprechaun Treasure Hunt

1. I'm a little leprechaun,
As crazy as can be
I've hidden a chest full
of _____,
But you must look
carefully.

2. I'm not here.
Where did I go?
Check the _____
And soon you will know!

3. Put on a smile.
Blink one, two, three...
Turn around
And look by a _____.

4. Pretty clever,
Don't you think?
Run to the _____
As quick as a wink.

5. Not here. Not here.
Look high and low.
But check the _____
Before you go.

6. Good for you, my little friends.
This hunt is coming to an end.
Look under a _____
for your last clue.
It will tell you what to do.

7. Somewhere there's a _____
That's really neat.
If you figure this out,
You'll find the treat.

8. Spring has sprung.
You're a whiz.
This is where the treasure is.
Enjoy! Little Leprechaun.

Mother's Marvelous Munchies

Guess How Much I Love You
by Sam McBratney (Candlewick Press)

Little Nutbrown Hare and Big Nutbrown Hare compete to show the magnitude of their love for each other. Big Nutbrown Hare shows that his love is greater by outdoing whatever Little Nutbrown Hare does. The love between the two hares will make children appreciate the love they share with others.

Children will marvel as they make some of mother's favorite things. They will learn two types of poetry and mix together mother's marvelous munchies.

Activity
Love Poem

Activity
My Mother

Chant
"Marvelous Munchies"

Cooking Experience
Mother's Marvelous Munchies

Related Literature

Are You My Mother? by P. D. Eastman (Random House)
Celebrating Mother's Day: Mom's Memory Book by Sandi Hill (Creative Teaching Press)
The Mother's Day Mice by Eve Bunting (Houghton Mifflin)
What Mommies Do Best/What Daddies Do Best by Laura Numeroff (Simon & Schuster)

Mother's Marvelous Munchies

Math Skill
- measuring

Name _____

I think this recipe is

Recipe

Ingredients
1 tablespoon each of the
following ingredients:
- O-shaped cereal
- peanuts
- almonds
- unshelled sunflower
  seeds
- Kix Cereal®
- mini-marshmallows
- honey

Utensils and Supplies
- measuring spoons
- plastic cup
- plastic spoon

Put in a plastic cup 1 tablespoon of each dry ingredient. Add 1 tablespoon honey, and stir.

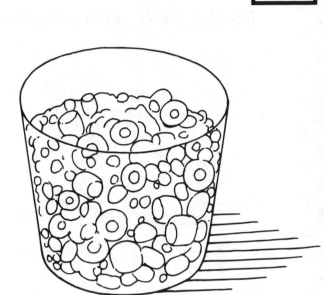

Marvelous Munchies
(chant rhythmically)

Mother's Marvelous Munchies
Make me happy as happy can be.
And whenever she makes them I let out a shout,
'Cause I know that she makes them for me.

Mother's Marvelous Munchies Recipe Cards

1. Put in a plastic cup 1 tablespoon each of O-shaped cereal, peanuts, almonds, unshelled sunflower seeds, Kix Cereal®, and mini-marshmallows.

2. Add 1 tablespoon honey.

3. Stir.

4. Munch on your munchies.

Mother's Marvelous Munchies

Love Poem

Give each child an **I Love You Poem (page 70)** and a piece of **blank paper.** Read the poem together, and invite children to write on each blank line a word that describes their mother. Ask children to place the blank paper vertically and draw a picture of their mother. Collect each child's poem and picture. Use glue to mount each child's work on a piece of **12" x 18" (30.5 cm x 46 cm) construction paper,** and display the papers in class.

My Mother

Have the class brainstorm words that begin with the letters in *MOTHER.* Give each child a copy of the **My Mother reproducible (page 71).** Ask children to use each letter of *MOTHER* to write a sentence that begins with the corresponding letter. For example, children could write *My mom is great!* for the letter *M.* Invite children to share their completed poem with the class and then take it home to their mother.

I Love You Poem

My mom likes to _____.
  My mom likes to play.
She also likes to _____.
  She is great in every way.

I like the way Mom _____.
  I like the way she shares.
She always tries to _____.
  And I know she really cares.

My mom is really_____.
  She's _____, yes, it's true.
That's why I want to tell you, Mom,
  Just how much I love you.

Love,

_____

My Mother

Name _____

M _____ .

O _____ .

T _____ .

H _____ .

E _____ .

R _____ .

Nifty Noodles

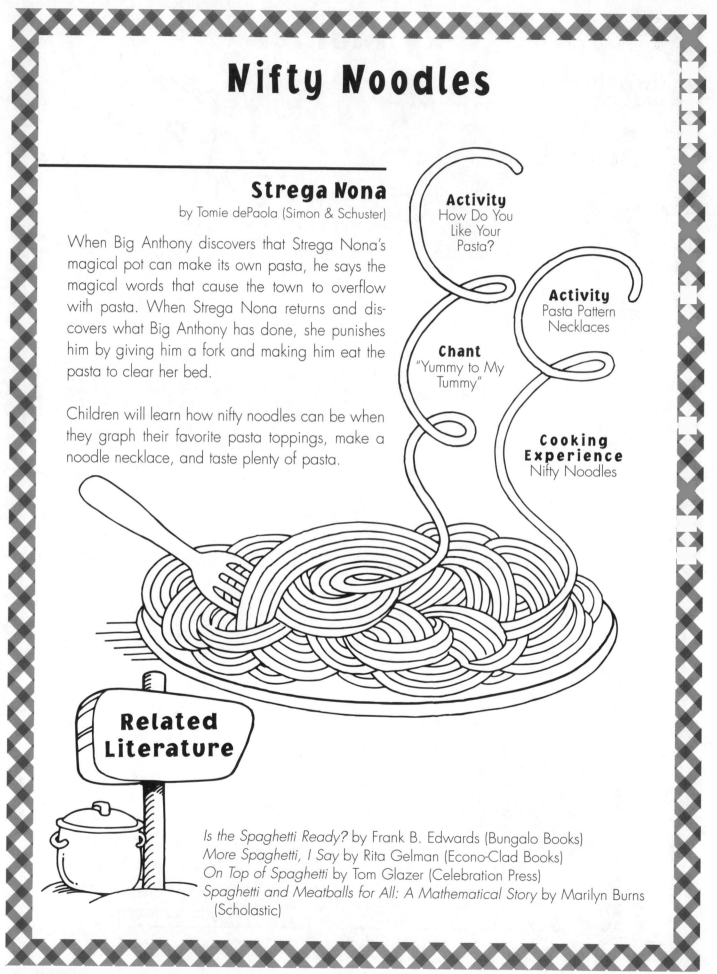

Strega Nona
by Tomie dePaola (Simon & Schuster)

When Big Anthony discovers that Strega Nona's magical pot can make its own pasta, he says the magical words that cause the town to overflow with pasta. When Strega Nona returns and discovers what Big Anthony has done, she punishes him by giving him a fork and making him eat the pasta to clear her bed.

Children will learn how nifty noodles can be when they graph their favorite pasta toppings, make a noodle necklace, and taste plenty of pasta.

Activity
How Do You Like Your Pasta?

Activity
Pasta Pattern Necklaces

Chant
"Yummy to My Tummy"

Cooking Experience
Nifty Noodles

Related Literature

Is the Spaghetti Ready? by Frank B. Edwards (Bungalo Books)
More Spaghetti, I Say by Rita Gelman (Econo-Clad Books)
On Top of Spaghetti by Tom Glazer (Celebration Press)
Spaghetti and Meatballs for All: A Mathematical Story by Marilyn Burns (Scholastic)

Nifty Noodles

Math Skill
- comparing

I think this recipe is

Recipe

Ingredients
- 1 cup variety of cooked noodles
- 1 tablespoon marinara sauce
- 1 tablespoon Italian dressing
- 1 teaspoon parmesan cheese

Utensils and Supplies
- measuring cup
- paper plate
- measuring spoons
- plastic fork

Place 1 cup cooked noodles on a paper plate. Separate the noodles into three piles. Pour 1 tablespoon marinara sauce on one pile. Pour 1 tablespoon Italian dressing on the second pile. Sprinkle 1 teaspoon parmesan cheese on the third pile. Enjoy!

Yummy to My Tummy
(chant rhythmically)

Have some nifty noodles.
They are yummy as can be:
Egg noodles, elbow, and rigatoni.

Linguine with marinara,
And shells with parmesan . . .
Then there's vermicelli.
The list goes on and on.

Toss some noodles in dressing,
Or stir them into cheese.
I just love my noodles.
May I have some, please?
Yummy to my tummy!

Nifty Noodles Recipe Cards

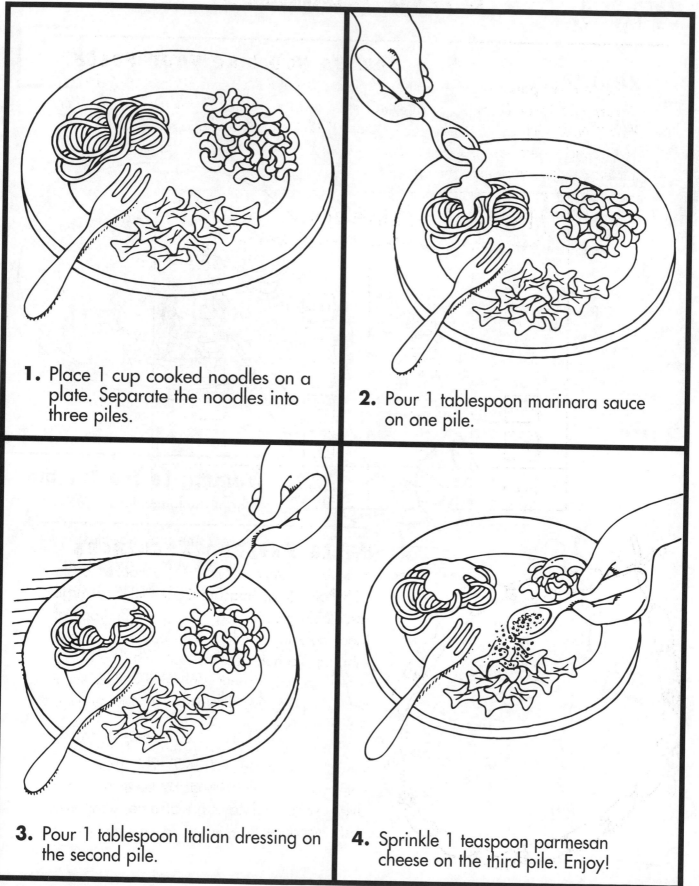

1. Place 1 cup cooked noodles on a plate. Separate the noodles into three piles.

2. Pour 1 tablespoon marinara sauce on one pile.

3. Pour 1 tablespoon Italian dressing on the second pile.

4. Sprinkle 1 teaspoon parmesan cheese on the third pile. Enjoy!

Nifty Noodles

How Do You Like Your Pasta?

Draw on **chart paper** a graph with four columns. Label the columns *Plain*, *With Marinara Sauce*, *With Italian Dressing*, and *With Cheese*, and title the graph *How Do You Like Your Pasta?* Write each child's name on a separate **1" (2.5 cm) paper square**, and place **tape** on the back of the squares. Ask children to place their square on the graph to show their favorite way to eat pasta.

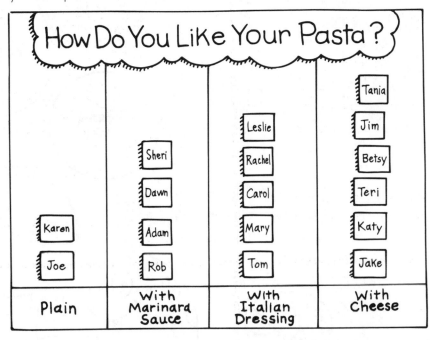

How Do You Like Your Pasta?

Plain	With Marinara Sauce	With Italian Dressing	With Cheese
			Tania
			Jim
		Leslie	Betsy
	Sheri	Rachel	Teri
	Dawn	Carol	Katy
Karen	Adam	Mary	Jake
Joe	Rob	Tom	

Pasta Pattern Necklaces

In advance, place a handful of **uncooked pasta with holes** (e.g., macaroni, penne) in a **large resealable plastic bag**. Add **2 or 3 drops of food coloring** and **1 tablespoon (15 mL) rubbing alcohol**. Seal the bag, and shake it to coat the pasta. Repeat this process with additional pieces of pasta and different colors. Lay the pasta flat on **newspaper** to dry overnight. Give each child a handful of colored pasta and a piece of **yarn**. Invite children to string their pasta in a pattern on their yarn. Tie together the ends of each child's yarn, and invite children to wear their pasta "necklace."

Oliver the Octopus

My Very Own Octopus
by Bernard Most (Harcourt)

While relaxing at the beach, a young boy dreams about having a pet octopus. He thinks about the many benefits of having an octopus as a pet. The boy imagines an octopus could help him clean his room, help him shovel snow, play baseball with him, clear the table, pick apples that could last ten years, and beat anybody in a snowball fight. Children will relate to this boy and his desire to have a pet.

Children do not need to go to the ocean to find an octopus. They will make several octopus friends when they make a paper octopus and draw an ocean scene. Children will watch Oliver the Octopus "curl up" when they cook their tasty hot dog treat.

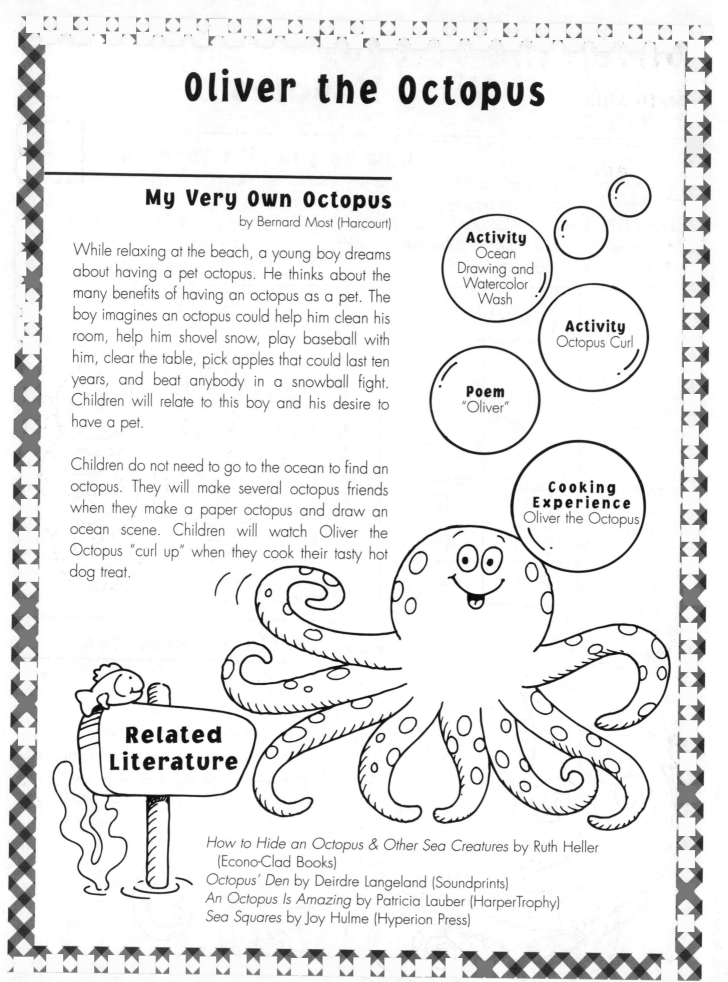

Activity
Ocean Drawing and Watercolor Wash

Activity
Octopus Curl

Poem
"Oliver"

Cooking Experience
Oliver the Octopus

Related Literature

How to Hide an Octopus & Other Sea Creatures by Ruth Heller (Econo-Clad Books)
Octopus' Den by Deirdre Langeland (Soundprints)
An Octopus Is Amazing by Patricia Lauber (HarperTrophy)
Sea Squares by Joy Hulme (Hyperion Press)

Oliver the Octopus

Math Skill
• making fractions (fourths)

I think this recipe is ☐

Recipe

Ingredients
• 1 hot dog
• catsup

Utensils and Supplies
• Crock-Pot® or hot plate and saucepan with lid
• plastic knife
• sharp knife (adult use only)
• tongs
• paper plate

Ask an adult to heat water to a boil in a Crock-Pot or saucepan. Use a plastic knife to cut the bottom half of a hot dog lengthwise into four equal parts, keeping the top half whole. Ask an adult to use a sharp knife to again cut each of the four "legs" in half lengthwise. Have an adult gently place the hot dog into the boiling water and cover the pot or pan with a lid. Let the hot dog cook until the ends are curled up tight. Have an adult use tongs to remove the hot dog and place it on a paper plate. Use catsup to make a face for the "octopus."

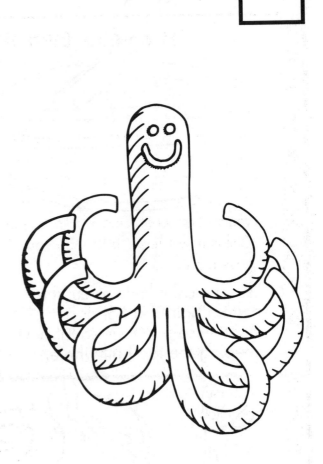

Oliver

Oliver the octopus
Has legs quite squiggly and squirrelly.
He bounces about in an ocean of red,
But he won't stay long, most assuredly.

Oliver the Octopus Recipe Cards

1. Use a plastic knife to cut the bottom half of a hot dog lengthwise into four equal parts, keeping the top half whole.

2. Ask an adult to use a sharp knife to again cut each of the four "legs" in half lengthwise.

3. Have an adult gently place the hot dog into the boiling water. Cover the pot with a lid. Let the hot dog cook until the ends are curled up tight.

4. Have an adult use tongs to remove the hot dog and place it on a plate. Use catsup to make a face for the "octopus."

Oliver the Octopus

Ocean Drawing and Watercolor Wash

Give each child a piece of **white construction paper, watercolor paints,** a **paintbrush,** and a **cup of water.** Have children use crayons to draw a picture of sea creatures. Invite them to dip their paintbrush in water and then paint over their crayon picture with watercolor paints in different colors of the ocean. Have children dip their paintbrush into the water each time they use a new color of paint. Once the paint is dry, collect the papers, use **tape** to combine them into one "mural," and display it on a bulletin board titled *Our Ocean.*

Octopus Curl

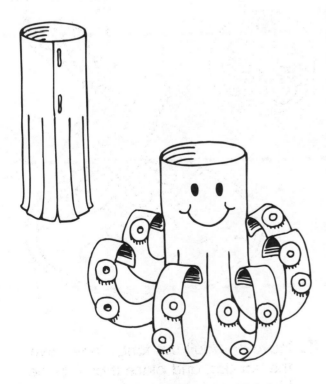

Give each child an **Octopus reproducible (page 80)** and a handful of **O-shaped cereal.** Have children color the reproducible and then cut along the dotted lines. Fold each child's paper so the strips ("legs") on both ends of the paper overlap, and **staple** together the top of the octopus and the overlapping legs (as shown). Show children how to wrap each strip around a pencil to curl the legs. Invite them to glue cereal to each leg to make "tentacles."

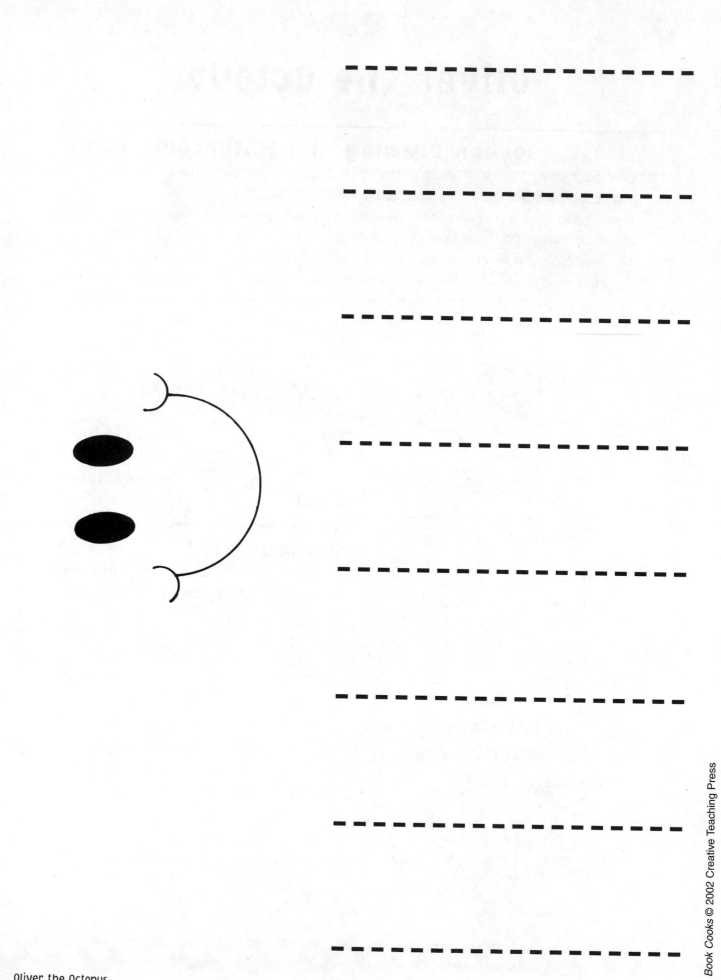

Purple Cow

Harold and the Purple Crayon
by Crockett Johnson (HarperCollins)

One evening, Harold decides to go for a walk. Harold brings his purple crayon, which he uses to draw things such as the moon, a dragon, a picnic, and a bed to sleep in when he gets tired. Watch children's imaginations go wild when they think of adventures they too can draw with a purple crayon.

Children will paint with purple paint, brainstorm *p* words, and drink a purple drink for some "punchy" purple fun.

Activity
P Words

Activity
Purple Pictures

Chant
"Have You Ever Seen a Purple Cow?"

Cooking Experience
Purple Cow

Related Literature

Harold's Fairy Tale: Further Adventures with the Purple Crayon
by Crockett Johnson (HarperTrophy)
Hello, Red Fox by Eric Carle (Simon & Schuster)

Purple Cow

Math Skill
- making fractions (halves)

Name _____

I think this recipe is [ ]

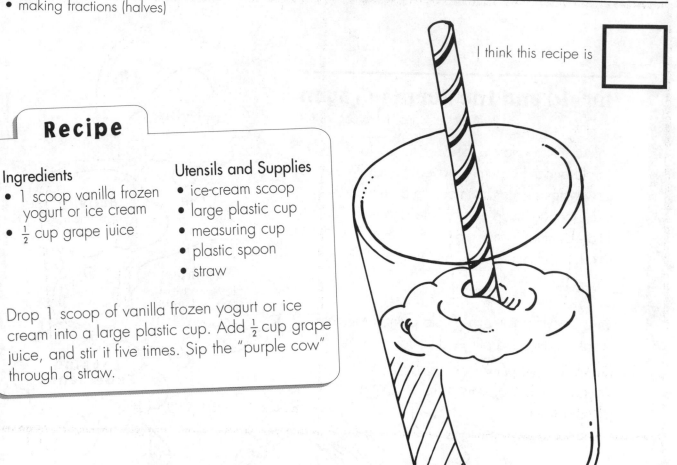

Recipe

Ingredients
- 1 scoop vanilla frozen yogurt or ice cream
- $\frac{1}{2}$ cup grape juice

Utensils and Supplies
- ice-cream scoop
- large plastic cup
- measuring cup
- plastic spoon
- straw

Drop 1 scoop of vanilla frozen yogurt or ice cream into a large plastic cup. Add $\frac{1}{2}$ cup grape juice, and stir it five times. Sip the "purple cow" through a straw.

Have You Ever Seen a Purple Cow?
(chant rhythmically)

Have you ever seen a purple cow?
Have you ever tried to eat one?
Just mix some grape juice with vanilla ice cream,
And you're sure to have some fun.

Purple Cow Recipe Cards

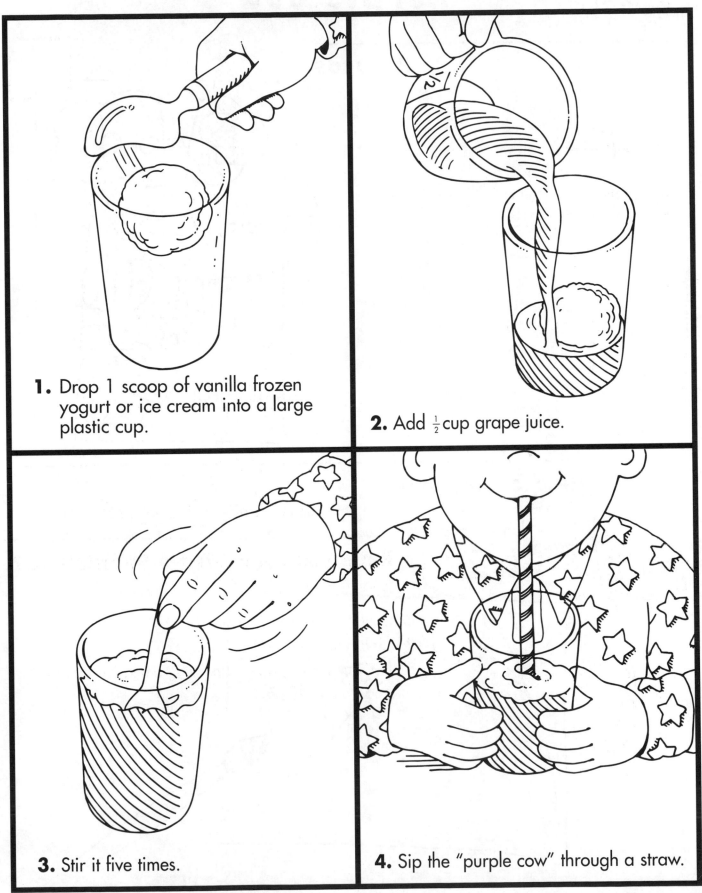

1. Drop 1 scoop of vanilla frozen yogurt or ice cream into a large plastic cup.

2. Add $\frac{1}{2}$ cup grape juice.

3. Stir it five times.

4. Sip the "purple cow" through a straw.

Purple Cow

P Words

Ask children to brainstorm words that begin with the letter *p*. Record their responses on the board or **chart paper**. Give each child a piece of **drawing paper**. Have children title their paper *P Words*. Ask children to choose words from the class list and write them on their paper. Invite children to illustrate each word.

Purple Pictures

Give each child a **mixing tray, red and blue tempera paint**, a **paintbrush**, and a piece of **drawing paper**. Invite children to mix together the red and blue paint to make purple. Then, have children paint a "purple picture" about an adventure they would like to have.

Quality Quilt

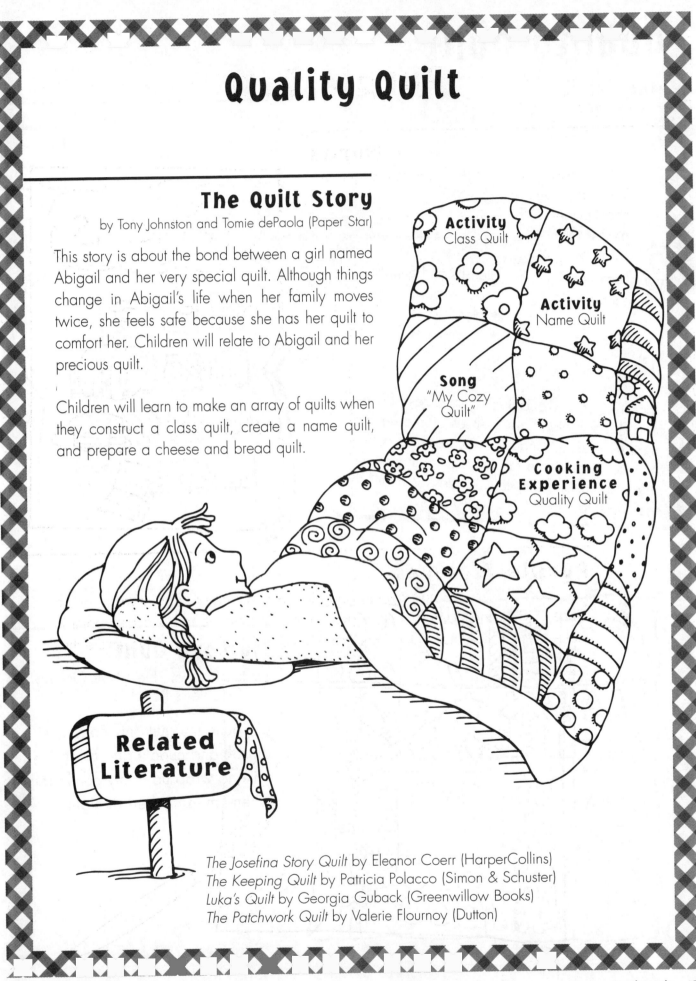

The Quilt Story

by Tony Johnston and Tomie dePaola (Paper Star)

This story is about the bond between a girl named Abigail and her very special quilt. Although things change in Abigail's life when her family moves twice, she feels safe because she has her quilt to comfort her. Children will relate to Abigail and her precious quilt.

Children will learn to make an array of quilts when they construct a class quilt, create a name quilt, and prepare a cheese and bread quilt.

Activity
Class Quilt

Activity
Name Quilt

Song
"My Cozy Quilt"

Cooking Experience
Quality Quilt

Related Literature

The Josefina Story Quilt by Eleanor Coerr (HarperCollins)
The Keeping Quilt by Patricia Polacco (Simon & Schuster)
Luka's Quilt by Georgia Guback (Greenwillow Books)
The Patchwork Quilt by Valerie Flournoy (Dutton)

Quality Quilt

Math Skill
• patterning

Name _____

I think this recipe is [ ]

Recipe

Ingredients
• 2 slices of yellow cheese
• 2 slices of white cheese
• 1 piece of bread

Utensils and Supplies
• paper plate
• plastic knife
• toaster oven (optional)

Place two yellow and two white slices of cheese on a paper plate. Cut the slices of cheese into small squares. Arrange the squares in a pattern on a piece of bread to create a "quilt." As an option, place the quilt in a toaster oven until the cheese melts.

My Cozy Quilt
(to the tune of "Here We Go 'Round the Cobbler's Bench")

My quilt, my quilt, my cozy quilt
all soft and cuddly and bright.
I like to wrap up in my comfy quilt
when I'm in my bed at night.

Quality Quilt Recipe Cards

1. Place two yellow and two white slices of cheese on a paper plate.

2. Cut the slices of cheese into small squares.

3. Arrange the squares in a pattern on a piece of bread to create a "quilt."

4. Nibble your yummy "quilt."

Quality Quilt

Class Quilt

Give each child a square piece of **9" (23 cm) paper.** Have children draw a picture that represents their favorite activity. Collect the papers, use **tape** to make a class "quilt," and display the quilt on a bulletin board titled *Our Class Quilt*. Invite children to point to their quilt piece and explain their picture to the class.

Name Quilt

Give each child a **Graph Paper reproducible (page 89).** Have children write their name in the boxes, starting in the top left box, one letter per box. Have them continue to write the letters of their name, in order, in the remaining boxes. Ask children to draw the same color and pattern in all the boxes that contain the same letters. For example, a child named Kim might draw green dots in all the boxes with the letter *K*, yellow spirals in all the boxes with the letter *i*, and blue lines in all the boxes with the letter *m*. Display the completed "name quilts" on a bulletin board.

Graph Paper

Rudie the Reindeer

Olive, the Other Reindeer
by J. Otto Seibold and Vivian Walsh (Chronicle Books)

Not all reindeers look the same in this special story. A dog named Olive thinks she must be a reindeer when she hears the famous reindeer song. Olive sets off to be with the "other" reindeer, and soon her adventure begins.

Children will recreate a reindeer using their handprints and footprints, make bags of munchies to give to any reindeer who happens to be near, and make a delicious reindeer out of a large rice cake.

Activity
Reindeer Prints

Activity
Reindeer Munchies Bag

Chant
"Little Reindeer"

Cooking Experience
Rudie the Reindeer

Related Literature

Rudolph the Red-Nosed Reindeer by Robert L. May (Applewood Books)
Triplet Trouble and the Runaway Reindeer by Debbie Dadey (Scholastic)
The Wild Christmas Reindeer by Jan Brett (Philomel)

Rudie the Reindeer

Math Skill
- counting

Name _____

I think this recipe is ☐

Recipe

Ingredients
- 1 tablespoon caramel sauce
- 1 large rice cake
- 2 Hershey® kisses
- 2 pretzel twists
- 1 maraschino cherry

Utensils and Supplies
- measuring spoon
- plastic knife
- paper plate

Spread 1 tablespoon caramel sauce on a rice cake. Add two Hershey® kisses to make "eyes." Add two pretzels to make "antlers." Place a cherry in the middle to make a "nose."

Little Reindeer
(chant rhythmically)

Spread a little caramel
On a crunchy rice cake.
Add two kisses for his eyes.
Two pretzels make the antlers,
And a cherry for his nose . . .
What a wonderful surprise!

Rudie the Reindeer Recipe Cards

1. Spread 1 tablespoon caramel sauce on a rice cake.

2. Add two Hershey® kisses to make "eyes."

3. Add two pretzels to make "antlers."

4. Place a cherry in the middle to make a "nose."

Book Cooks © 2002 Creative Teaching Press

Rudie the Reindeer

Reindeer Prints

Have each child bring in a **white T-shirt,** or give each child a piece of **white construction paper.** Paint the bottom of each child's foot with **brown fabric paint** (for a shirt) or **brown tempera paint** (for paper). Have each child press his or her foot on the shirt or paper (with the heel facing down) to make a "reindeer face." Paint each child's hands with a **different shade of brown paint,** and have children place their hands above their footprint to make "antlers." Use scissors to cut **sponges** in the shape of holly leaves. Have children dip a sponge in **green paint** and then stamp their shirt or paper. Ask them to dip their thumb into **red paint** and then place their thumb on the holly leaves to make berries. Have children use glue to attach a red **pom-pom or puff ball** to their footprint to make a nose. Invite them to glue **large wiggly eyes** on their shirt or paint eyes on their paper.

Reindeer Munchies Bag

Give each child a **paper bag** and a piece of **brown construction paper.** Have children fold the top corners of their bag into a triangle and then fold the triangle down to make an upside-down triangle. Have them trace both their hands on the brown paper, cut out their tracings, and then glue their cutouts to the top of the bag to make antlers. Ask children to draw eyes and a nose. Have children glue a **Reindeer Munchies poem (page 94)** to the back of their bag. Give children a handful of "reindeer munchies" **(birdseed)** to put in their bag. Read the poem with the class.

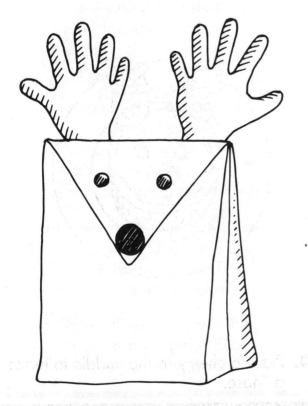

Reindeer Munchies

This bag of
Reindeer Munchies
is a rather special treat
for hungry little reindeer who
come with prancing feet.

Just toss some up
onto the roof
before you go to bed.
They'll be content to nibble
while Santa's gone from his sled.

But, if Reindeer Munchies are
not your thing,
feed it to the birdies, and
listen to them sing.

Enjoy the gladness that giving
can bring, and enjoy a
Happy New Year!

This bag of
Reindeer Munchies
is a rather special treat
for hungry little reindeer who
come with prancing feet.

Just toss some up
onto the roof
before you go to bed.
They'll be content to nibble
while Santa's gone from his sled.

But, if Reindeer Munchies are
not your thing,
feed it to the birdies, and
listen to them sing.

Enjoy the gladness that giving
can bring, and enjoy a
Happy New Year!

This bag of
Reindeer Munchies
is a rather special treat
for hungry little reindeer who
come with prancing feet.

Just toss some up
onto the roof
before you go to bed.
They'll be content to nibble
while Santa's gone from his sled.

But, if Reindeer Munchies are
not your thing,
feed it to the birdies, and
listen to them sing.

Enjoy the gladness that giving
can bring, and enjoy a
Happy New Year!

This bag of
Reindeer Munchies
is a rather special treat
for hungry little reindeer who
come with prancing feet.

Just toss some up
onto the roof
before you go to bed.
They'll be content to nibble
while Santa's gone from his sled.

But, if Reindeer Munchies are
not your thing,
feed it to the birdies, and
listen to them sing.

Enjoy the gladness that giving
can bring, and enjoy a
Happy New Year!

Sunflower Yellow

Sunflower House
by Eve Bunting (Harcourt)

When a little boy plants some sunflower seeds that grow into a circle of large flowers, the boy and his friends use their imagination to turn their sunflower playhouse into different things. When the beautiful sunflowers die at the end of the summer, the boy collects seeds from the dying flowers to sow for next summer's flowers. Children will be eager to make their own sunflower playhouse just like the little boy.

Children will learn all the special things about a sunflower when they use sunflower seeds to help solve math equations and practice counting. Then, they will make a scrumptious sunflower treat.

Activity
Sunflower Math

Activity
Sunflower Seed Counting

Song
"Sunflower Yellow"

Cooking Experience
Sunflower Yellow

Related Literature

A Field of Sunflowers by Neil Johnson (Econo-Clad Books)
Sunflower Sal by Janet S. Anderson (Albert Whitman)

Sunflower Yellow

Math Skill
- estimating

Name _____

I think this recipe is

Recipe

Ingredients
- 1 large rice cake
- 2 tablespoons caramel sauce or peanut butter
- $\frac{1}{2}$ banana
- $\frac{1}{4}$ cup unshelled sunflower seeds
- 1 green licorice whip

Utensils and Supplies
- paper plate
- measuring spoon
- plastic knife
- measuring cup

Spread 2 tablespoons caramel sauce or peanut butter on a rice cake. Estimate how many circles you can cut from half of a banana, and then cut the banana into circles. Arrange the circles around the edge of the rice cake. Sprinkle $\frac{1}{4}$ cup sunflower seeds in the center, and add a green licorice whip to make a "stem."

Sunflower Yellow
(to the tune of "Baa, Baa, Black Sheep")

Sunflower yellow,
Standing in the sun,
Soon you will be eaten
After all the work is done.

Sunflower Yellow Recipe Cards

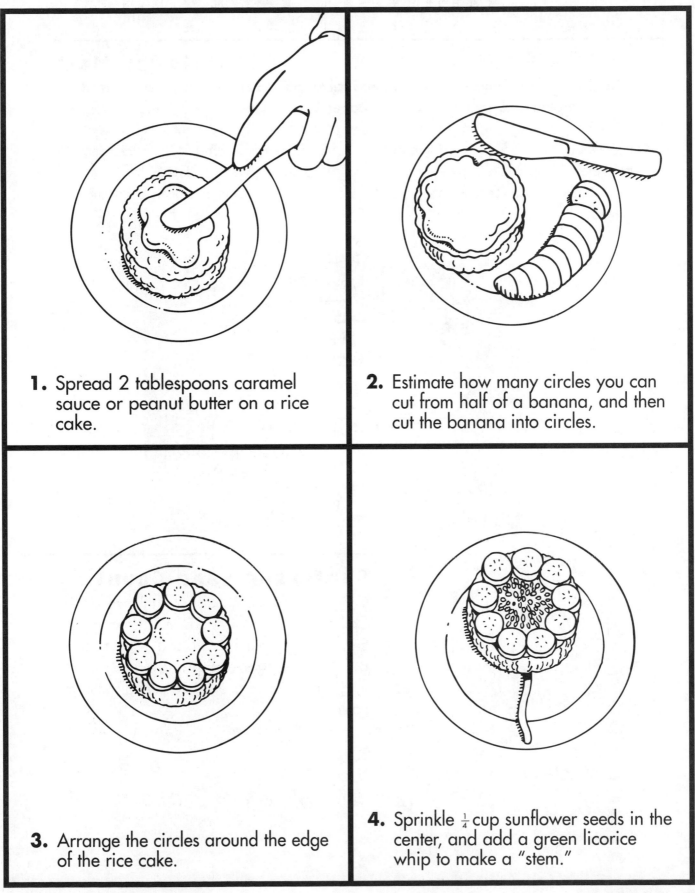

1. Spread 2 tablespoons caramel sauce or peanut butter on a rice cake.

2. Estimate how many circles you can cut from half of a banana, and then cut the banana into circles.

3. Arrange the circles around the edge of the rice cake.

4. Sprinkle $\frac{1}{4}$ cup sunflower seeds in the center, and add a green licorice whip to make a "stem."

Sunflower Yellow

Sunflower Math

Give each child a **Sunflower Math reproducible (page 99)**, **24 sunflower seeds**, and a piece of **brown and yellow construction paper**. Invite children to use the seeds to help them solve the math problems and then write their answers. Have them cut out the circle and glue it to their brown paper. Tell children to cut out petals from yellow construction paper and glue the petals to the circle to make a "sunflower." To extend the activity, invite children to glue their seeds on the reproducible to illustrate each math problem and then count the total number of seeds on their paper.

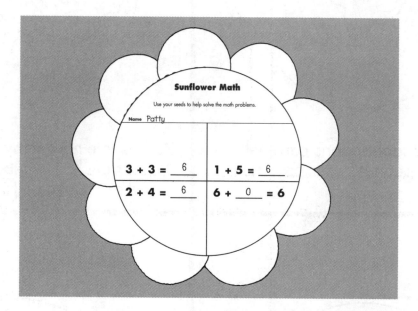

Sunflower Seed Counting

Give each child a handful of **sunflower seeds**. Explain how to place seeds in different groups. Encourage children to group and count the seeds by ones, twos, fives, and tens. To extend the activity, plant the seeds and record their growth on a calendar.

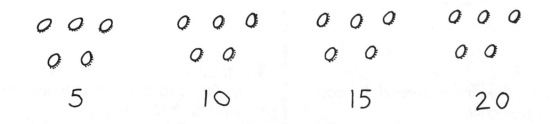

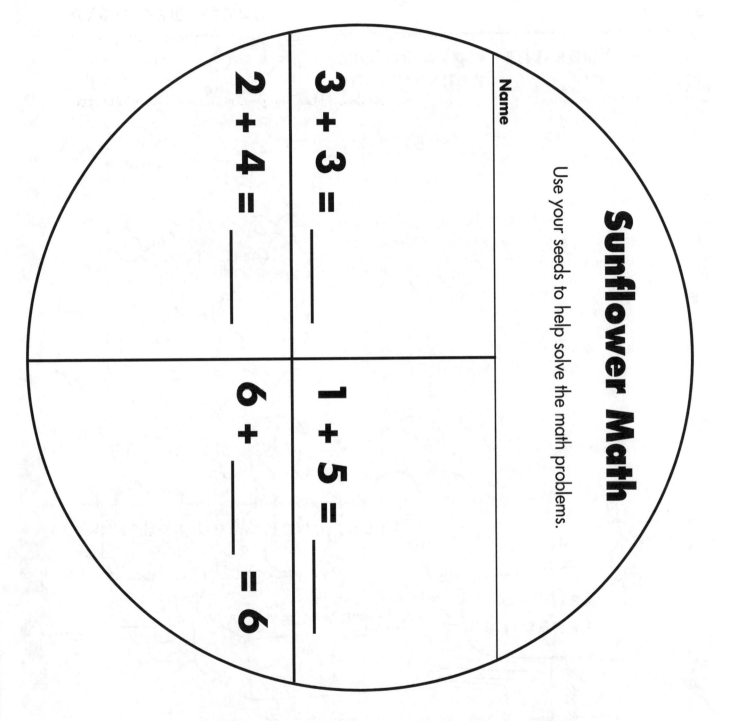

Sunflower Math

Name

Use your seeds to help solve the math problems.

3 + 3 = _____

2 + 4 = _____

1 + 5 = _____

6 + _____ = 6

Terrific Turkey Taco

'Twas the Night Before Thanksgiving
by Dav Pilkey (Orchard Books)

'Twas the day before Thanksgiving, and a group of students drove in a bus to Farmer MacNuggett's farm. While on the farm, the children befriended some turkeys and rescued them from their death. The children snuck the turkeys on the bus and brought them home. They introduced the turkeys to their families, and each family enjoyed a turkey-free Thanksgiving feast. Children will love the fast-paced rhyme in this story.

Children will make tasty taco treats, complete a turkey taco survey, and come up with their own terrific taco recipes.

Activity
Tasty Turkey Taco Recipes

Activity
Turkey Taco Survey

Chant
"Just Right!"

Cooking Experience
Terrific Turkey Taco

Related Literature

All About Turkeys by Jim Arnosky (Scholastic)
Gracias: The Thanksgiving Turkey by Joy Cowley (Scholastic)
A Turkey for Thanksgiving by Eve Bunting (Clarion Books)
The Turkey Saves the Day by Shelagh Canning (Troll Communications)

Terrific Turkey Taco

Math Skill
• measuring

Name _____

I think this recipe is ☐

Recipe

Ingredients
• 1 flour tortilla
• $\frac{1}{2}$ cup cooked ground turkey
• 1 tablespoon shredded cheese
• $\frac{1}{4}$ cup shredded lettuce
• $\frac{1}{4}$ cup chopped tomatoes
• 1 tablespoon salsa

Utensils and Supplies
• paper plate
• measuring cups
• measuring spoons

Put $\frac{1}{2}$ cup cooked ground turkey on a tortilla. Add 1 tablespoon cheese, $\frac{1}{4}$ cup lettuce, and $\frac{1}{4}$ cup tomatoes to the tortilla. Pour 1 tablespoon salsa on top. Fold the tortilla in half.

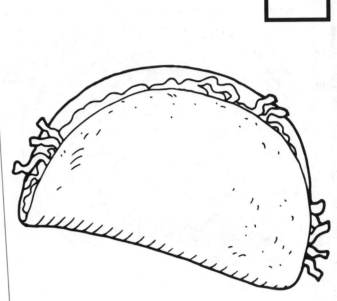

Just Right!
(chant rhythmically)

Terrific turkey taco,
All rolled up tight,
With some cheese and salsa
It tastes just right!

Terrific Turkey Taco Recipe Cards

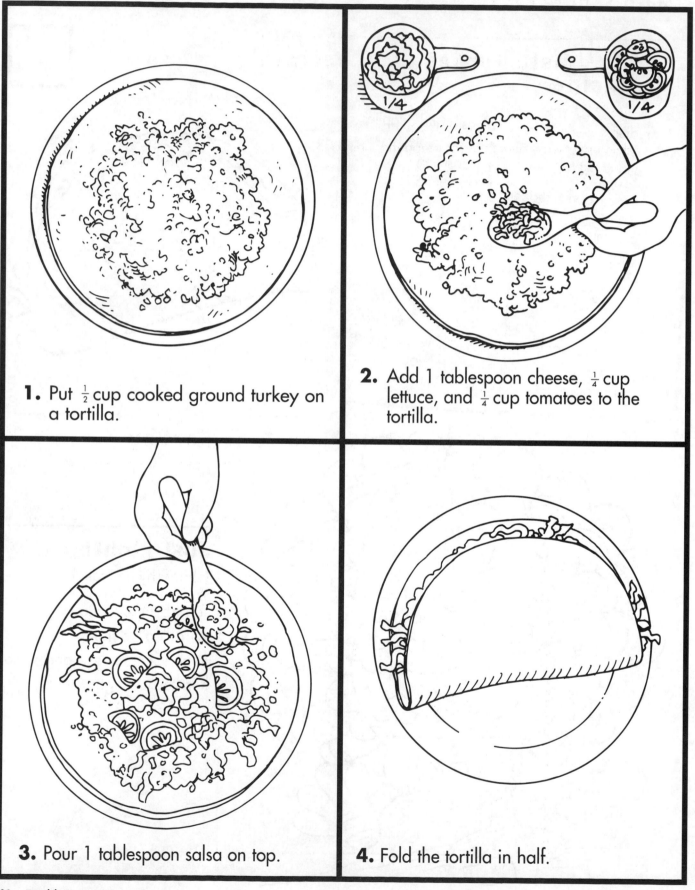

1. Put $\frac{1}{2}$ cup cooked ground turkey on a tortilla.

2. Add 1 tablespoon cheese, $\frac{1}{4}$ cup lettuce, and $\frac{1}{4}$ cup tomatoes to the tortilla.

3. Pour 1 tablespoon salsa on top.

4. Fold the tortilla in half.

Terrific Turkey Taco

Tasty Turkey Taco Recipes

Give each child a **large index card.** Invite children to create their own tasty turkey taco recipe. Have children draw the ingredients they would use in their taco. Encourage children to write directions for preparing their taco.

Turkey Taco Survey

Draw a T chart on **chart paper.** Label one column *Yes* and the other column *No*, and title the chart *Do You Like Turkey Tacos?* Ask each child to place a tally mark in the appropriate column. Encourage the class to count the tally marks and compare the total number of marks in each column.

Ugly Bugs

How Many Bugs in a Box? A Pop-Up Counting Book

by David A. Carter (Simon & Schuster)

This pop-up book has a brightly colored box on each page. Each box contains different bugs. Children will enjoy opening the boxes and counting the bug surprise.

Children will observe the attributes of different bugs, make a glue "bug" that clings to a window or wall, and create the ultimate ugly bug treat that they will be eager to eat.

Activity
Bugs! Bugs! Bugs!

Activity
Ugly Bug Cling

Song
"My Ugly Bug"

Cooking Experience
Ugly Bugs

Related Literature

The Icky Bug Alphabet Book by Jerry Pallotta (Econo-Clad Books)
The Ultimate Bug Book: A Unique Introduction to the World of Insects in Fabulous, Full-Color Pop-Ups by Luise Woelflein (Golden Books)

Ugly Bugs

Math Skill
• patterning

I think this recipe is ☐

Recipe

Ingredients
• 3 mini-muffins
• assortment of goodies (e.g., pretzel sticks, red imperials, licorice whips, shredded coconut, raisins, chocolate chips, mini-marshmallows)
• 1 scoop frosting

Utensils and Supplies
• spoon
• paper plate
• plastic knife

Place a scoop of frosting on a paper plate. Frost one side of three mini-muffins, and stick them together. Use frosting to attach goodies to make "legs," "eyes," and "antennae" for your "ugly bug." Add more goodies to make a pattern on the bug's body.

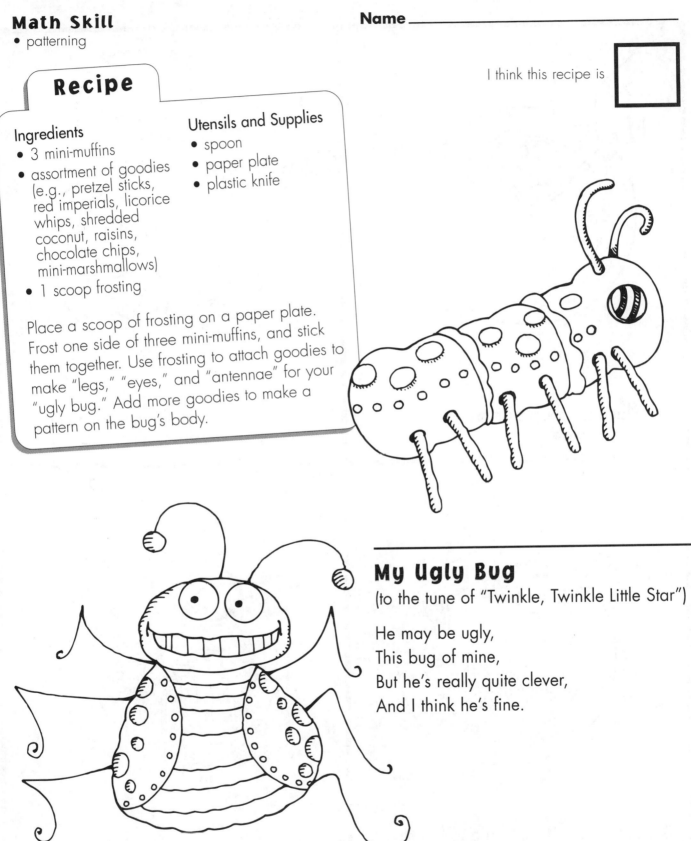

My Ugly Bug
(to the tune of "Twinkle, Twinkle Little Star")

He may be ugly,
This bug of mine,
But he's really quite clever,
And I think he's fine.

Ugly Bugs Recipe Cards

1. Place a scoop of frosting on a paper plate.

2. Frost one side of three mini-muffins, and stick them together.

3. Use frosting to attach goodies to make "legs," "eyes," and "antennae" for your "ugly bug."

4. Add more goodies to make a pattern on the bug's body.

Ugly Bugs

Bugs! Bugs! Bugs!

Invite children to bring **plastic bugs or insects** from home. Give each child a **magnifying glass,** and have children observe the attributes of each bug or insect. Have them sort the bugs and insects by common attributes.

Ugly Bug Cling

Give each child a piece of **waxed paper** and various containers of **colored glue.** Invite children to use the glue to make "bugs" on the waxed paper. When the glue dries, have children peel their bugs off the paper. Place the bugs on windows, and watch them "cling."

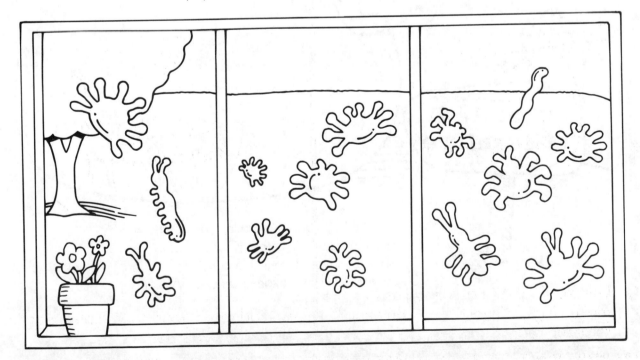

Vegetable Soup

Stone Soup
by Ann McGovern (Scholastic)

A very hungry man asks an old lady for some food. When she tells him she has no food to give him, the man convinces the old lady to make him a pot of soup with a stone. The man talks the old lady into adding some juicy beef bones, long thin carrots, yellow onions, and a bit of salt and pepper to the pot of stone soup.

Children will create their own vegetable fun when they learn how plants "eat," sort vegetables by edible parts, and make their own vegetable soup.

Activity
How Do Plants Eat?

Activity
Vegetable Sort

Song
"Tasty As Can Be"

Cooking Experience
Vegetable Soup

Related Literature

Growing Vegetable Soup by Lois Ehlert (Harcourt)
June 29, 1999 by David Wiesner (Clarion Books)
Tops & Bottoms by Janet Stevens (Harcourt)
We Can Eat the Plants by Rozanne Lanczak Williams (Creative Teaching Press)

Vegetable Soup

Math Skill
- measuring

I think this recipe is ☐

Recipe

Ingredients
- 2 cups water
- variety of cleaned and cut vegetables
- $\frac{1}{2}$ teaspoon vegetable bouillon

Utensils and Supplies
- Crock-Pot® or hot plate with saucepan and lid
- measuring cup
- measuring spoon
- mixing spoon
- bowl
- spoon

Fill a Crock-Pot or saucepan with 2 cups water. Add chopped vegetables. Add $\frac{1}{2}$ teaspoon vegetable bouillon, and stir. Ask an adult to turn on the Crock-Pot or heat the saucepan. Let the soup simmer until the vegetables are soft. Ask an adult to pour the soup into a bowl. Enjoy!

Tasty As Can Be
(to the tune of "Turkey in the Straw")

Oh, vegetable soup
Is as tasty as can be.
Made from roots, stems, leaves, seeds, and flowers
There'll be some for you and me.

If we're quick to share with others,
Then we'll end up having a lot.
So be sure that you come hungry,
And help fill our giant pot.

Vegetable Soup Recipe Cards

1. Fill a Crock-Pot® or saucepan with 2 cups water.

2. Add chopped vegetables. Add $\frac{1}{2}$ teaspoon vegetable bouillon. Stir.

3. Ask an adult to turn on the Crock-Pot or heat the saucepan.

4. Let the soup simmer until the vegetables are soft. Ask an adult to pour the soup into a bowl. Enjoy!

Vegetable Soup

How Do Plants Eat?

As a class, talk about plants and what makes them grow (sunlight, water, and soil). Explain that the roots of plants gather water and food from the soil and send it up through the plants' "veins" so all the parts of the plant get water and food. To show how this works, gather three **celery stalks with leaves,** three **plastic cups, water,** and **red, green, and blue food coloring.** Cut the celery stalks about 1" (2.5 cm) from the bottom of the main stalk. Tip up the bottom of a piece of celery, and show children the little holes (veins). Explain that those veins draw water and food up through the holes—just like when we drink from a straw. Place one stalk in a cup of red-tinted water, the second stalk in a cup of green-tinted water, and the third stalk in a cup of blue-tinted water. Wait a few hours, and then check the stalks. The tops of the leaves will begin to turn the same color as the water. Cut one of the stalks in half so children can see the colored water in the veins.

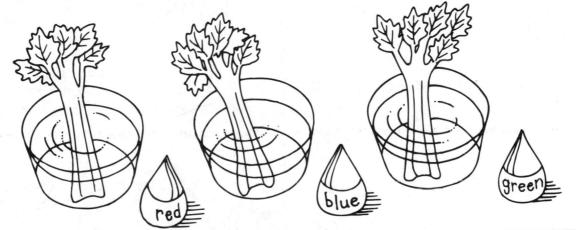

Vegetable Sort

Divide a large piece of **butcher paper** into five sections and label them as follows: *flowers, stems, roots, leaves,* and *seeds*. Give individual children different types of vegetables to sort by edible parts. Have children sort **broccoli, cauliflower, celery, asparagus, carrots, beets, onions, potatoes, ginger root, lettuce, spinach, corn,** and **peas.** Place the butcher paper on the floor, and have children place the vegetables on the butcher paper under the correct heading.

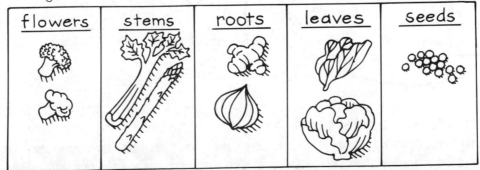

Washington's Cherry Pie

A Picture Book of George Washington

by David A. Adler (Holiday House)

George Washington's childhood, his career as a surveyor, and his life as the first president of the United States are shown in this picture book. Children will enjoy the cartoon-like characters that help explain the history of the United States of America.

Children will learn about the first president of the United States, create their own dollar bill, discuss the different jobs George Washington had, and smile with delight when they make a cherry pie surprise.

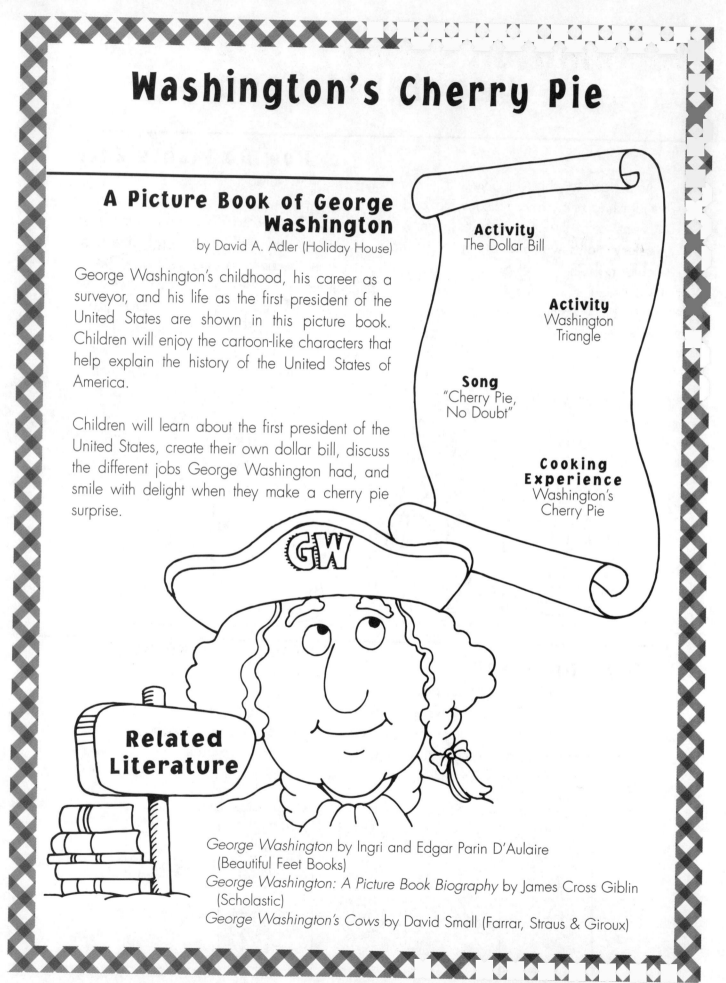

Activity
The Dollar Bill

Activity
Washington Triangle

Song
"Cherry Pie, No Doubt"

Cooking Experience
Washington's Cherry Pie

Related Literature

George Washington by Ingri and Edgar Parin D'Aulaire (Beautiful Feet Books)

George Washington: A Picture Book Biography by James Cross Giblin (Scholastic)

George Washington's Cows by David Small (Farrar, Straus & Giroux)

Washington's Cherry Pie

Math Skill
- counting

Name _____

I think this recipe is

Recipe

Ingredients
- 1 large graham cracker
- 1 large spoonful of cherry pie filling
- whipped cream

Utensils and Supplies
- resealable plastic bag
- clear plastic cup
- plastic spoon

Place one large graham cracker in a resealable plastic bag. Seal the bag, and smash it with your fist 20 times. Pour the crumbs into a clear plastic cup. Scoop 1 large spoonful of cherry pie filling into the cup. Add whipped cream on top.

Cherry Pie, No Doubt
(to the tune of "Row, Row, Row Your Boat")

Smash, smash, smash the bag,
Then pour the crumblies out.
Scoop some goo,
Then squirt the cream . . .
It's cherry pie, no doubt.

Washington's Cherry Pie Recipe Cards

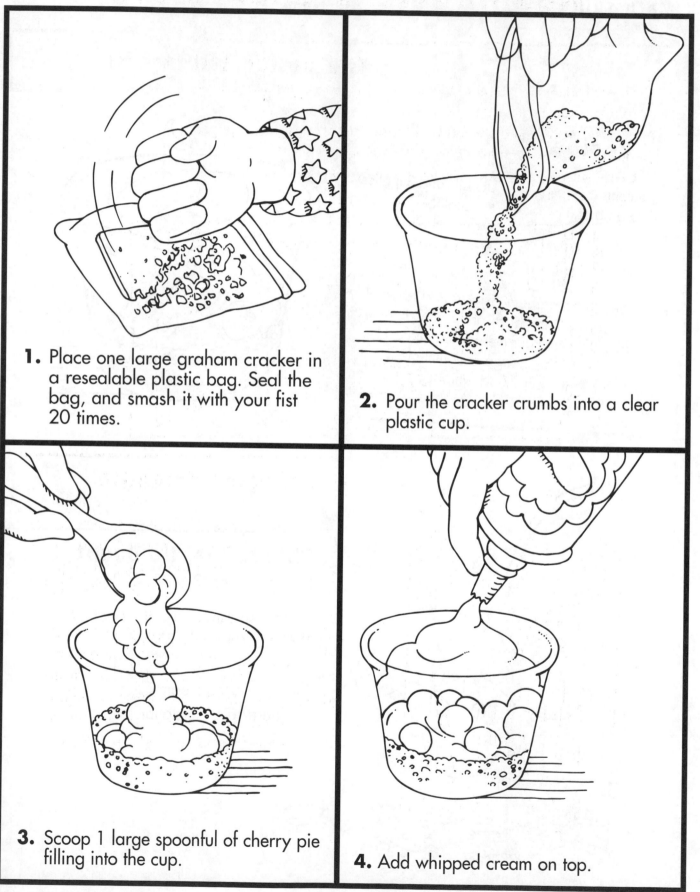

1. Place one large graham cracker in a resealable plastic bag. Seal the bag, and smash it with your fist 20 times.

2. Pour the cracker crumbs into a clear plastic cup.

3. Scoop 1 large spoonful of cherry pie filling into the cup.

4. Add whipped cream on top.

Washington's Cherry Pie

The Dollar Bill

Show children the picture of George Washington on a **dollar bill.** As a class, examine the other details found on both sides of the bill. Give each child a $2\frac{1}{2}$" x 6" (6.3 cm x 15 cm) strip of construction paper. Have children design their own dollar bill. Invite them to draw on the bill a picture of a president, themself, or anyone else. Invite children to share their bill with the class.

Washington Triangle

Give each child a **Washington Triangle reproducible (page 116)** and a piece of 6" x 18" (15 cm x 46 cm) paper. Discuss the different jobs George Washington had (e.g., surveyor, general, president). Ask children to point to the pictures of George Washington and name each job. Have them color and cut apart the pictures. Ask children to draw a background scene on their paper. Then, have them fold their paper into thirds and glue the edges together to create a triangle. Ask children to glue one picture on each side of their triangle.

Washington Triangle

Xs and Os

A Book of Hugs
by Dave Ross (HarperCollins)

This book explains different types of hugs that can be given. From the report card hug, to the lamp-post hug, children will love this "huggable" book.

Everyone needs a hug sometime. Children will draw pictures or write notes for loved ones, practice the topic of study with Tic-Tac-Toe Trivia, and "fall in love" with the yummy Xs and Os treat.

Activity
Love Notes

Activity
Tic-Tac-Toe Trivia

Poem
"Hugs and Kisses"

Cooking Experience
Xs and Os

Related Literature

A Book of Kisses by Dave Ross (HarperCollins)
A Kiss for Little Bear by Else Homelund Minarik (HarperCollins)
Toby's Holiday Hugs and Kisses by Cyndy Szekeres (Simon & Schuster)

Xs and Os

Math Skill
• making fractions (quarters)

Name _____

I think this recipe is ☐

Recipe

Ingredients
- 1 round chocolate or vanilla wafer
- softened cream cheese or white frosting
- chocolate decorator gel
- 4 chocolate chips

Utensils and Supplies
- plastic knife
- paper plate

Frost a round chocolate or vanilla wafer with softened cream cheese or white frosting. Use chocolate decorator gel to draw an X across the top of the wafer. Add a chocolate chip "kiss" to each fourth of the wafer.

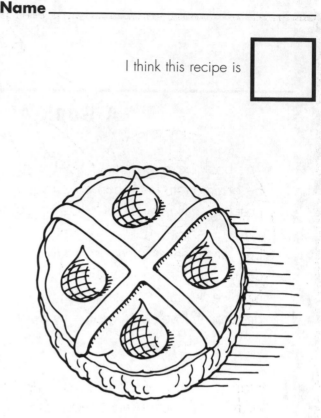

Hugs and Kisses

With Xs and Os,
As everyone knows,
A wonderful feeling grows down to your toes.
The O is a hug and the X is a kiss.
What could possibly be better than this?
OXOXOX

Xs and Os Recipe Cards

1. Frost a round chocolate or vanilla wafer with softened cream cheese or white frosting.

2. Use chocolate decorator gel to draw an X across the top of the wafer.

Gel

Chocolate Chips

3. Add a chocolate chip "kiss" to each quarter of the wafer.

4. Enjoy your "hug" and "kisses."

Xs and Os

Love Notes

Ask each child to write a note or draw a picture for someone he or she loves. Invite children to share their note or picture with the class and describe one special thing the person does. Have children give their note or picture to their loved one.

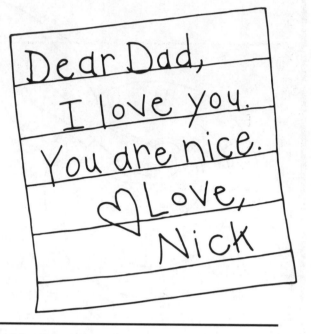

Tic-Tac-Toe Trivia

Prepare a **list of questions that relate to a current topic of study.** Divide the class into two teams, X and O. Draw a tic-tac-toe board on the chalkboard. Ask one member from the first team to answer a question. If the answer is correct, have that child write an X or O on the game board. If the child gives an incorrect response, invite one member from the other team to give an answer. Continue asking questions until one team gets tic-tac-toe.

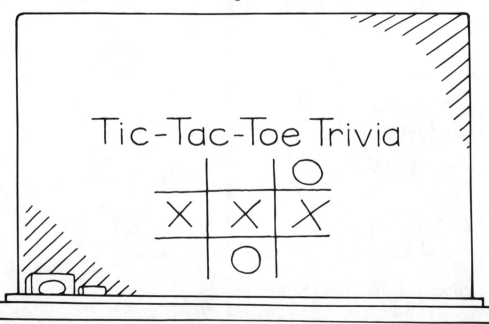

Yummy Yams

Yummers!
by James Marshall (Houghton Mifflin)

Emily Pig loves to eat, but Eugene Turtle thinks Emily could use some exercise. The two friends set off together to take a walk. On their walk, Emily and Eugene become hungry and keep stopping for food. Children will want to join Emily and Eugene on their "yummy" adventure.

Children will have "yam fun" as they observe a yam sprout roots, determine if classmates like yams or yogurt better, and prepare a sweet yam treat.

Activity
Sprout a Yam

Activity
Yams or Yogurt?

Chant
"Squishy and Light"

Cooking Experience
Yummy Yams

Related Literature

Yuck, a Love Story by Don Gillmor and Marie-Louise Gay (Stoddart Publishing)
Yummers Too: The Second Course by James Marshall (Houghton Mifflin)

Yummy Yams

Math Skill
- measuring

Name _____

I think this recipe is

Recipe

Ingredients
- $\frac{1}{2}$ precooked yam
- 1 tablespoon brown sugar
- 5 mini-marshmallows

Utensils and Supplies
- plastic knife
- aluminum foil
- measuring spoon
- plastic fork
- toaster oven (optional)

Peel the yam, and slice it into circles. Place the circles on a piece of aluminum foil. Sprinkle each circle with brown sugar. Top with five mini-marshmallows. If a toaster oven is available, lightly brown the yams.

Squishy and Light
(chant rhythmically)

Yams are yummy.
They're squishy and light.
Sprinkled with brown sugar,
They taste just right!

Book Cooks © 2002 Creative Teaching Press

Yummy Yams Recipe Cards

1. Peel the yam, and slice it into circles. Place the circles on a piece of aluminum foil.

2. Sprinkle each circle with brown sugar.

3. Top with five mini-marshmallows.

4. Enjoy your yummy yam!

Yummy Yams

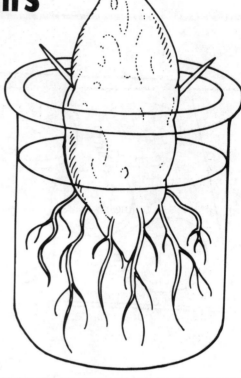

Sprout a Yam

Fill a jar half way with **water.** Submerge a **yam** in the water. Add **toothpicks** to the sides of the yam if needed to keep it afloat. Ask children to predict how long it will take for the yam to begin sprouting. Record their predictions on **chart paper.** Invite children to observe the yam daily, and record their observations on the chart paper.

Yams or Yogurt?

Draw a Venn diagram on a large piece of **construction paper.** Label one circle *Likes Yams* and the other circle *Likes Yogurt.* Title the diagram *Do You Like Yams or Yogurt?* Invite each child to write his or her name in the appropriate circle. If children like both yams and yogurt, have them write their name in the intersecting part of the circles. If they dislike both, have them write their name outside the circles.

Zebra Pudding

Ziggy the Zebra
by Libby Ellis (Piggy Toes Press)

Ziggy the Zebra learns a great lesson when he looks for his stripes. He wishes he were more like the other animals. When he realizes that the best thing to be is yourself, Ziggy earns his stripes.

Children will earn their "stripes" when they learn about sorting, graphing, and estimating. They will also learn about patterning as they use pudding to make zebra stripes.

Activity
Animal Cookie Sort

Activity
Animal Cookie Estimation

Chant
"Zebra Stripes"

Cooking Experience
Zebra Pudding

Related Literature

A Children's Zoo by Tana Hoban (Greenwillow Books)
Going to the Zoo by Tom Paxton (William Morrow & Company)
If I Ran the Zoo by Dr. Seuss (Random House)

Zebra Pudding

Math Skill
• patterning

Name _____

I think this recipe is

Recipe

Ingredients
• ½ cup premade chocolate pudding
• ½ cup premade vanilla pudding
• whipped cream
• 3 animal cookies

Utensils and Supplies
• clear plastic cup
• plastic spoon

Scoop alternating layers of chocolate and vanilla pudding into a cup. Add whipped cream to the top. Add three animal cookies. Enjoy your "zebra-stripe" pudding.

Zebra Stripes
(chant rhythmically)

Zebra pudding,
Yum, diddle-de-dum,
Black and white,
I'm sure you'll want some.

Add a squirt of cream on top,
Some animal cookies, too.
Then take a spoon and dig right in,
'Cause there's nothing more to do.

Yum, yum . . .
Diddle-de-dum.

Book Cooks © 2002 Creative Teaching Press

Zebra Pudding Recipe Cards

1. Scoop alternating layers of chocolate and vanilla pudding into a cup.

2. Add whipped cream to the top.

3. Add three animal cookies.

4. Enjoy your "zebra-stripe" pudding!

Zebra Pudding

Animal Cookie Sort

Give each child a handful of **animal cookies.** Invite children to sort the cookies by common attributes (e.g., lives in water, has fur) and count their total number of cookies. To extend the activity, give each child a Graph Paper reproducible (page 89), and invite children to graph the animals by common attributes.

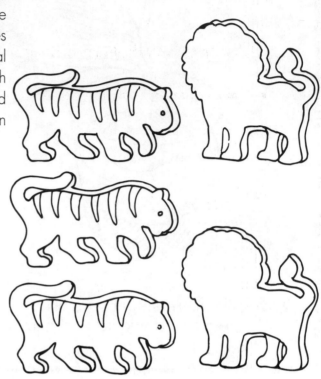

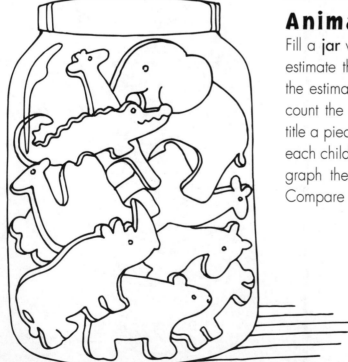

Animal Cookie Estimation

Fill a **jar** with **animal cookies,** and have children estimate the number of cookies in the jar. Record the estimations on **chart paper.** Invite the class to count the cookies together. To extend the activity, title a piece of chart paper *Does It Have Fur?* Give each child an animal cookie, and invite children to graph their animal by whether or not it has fur. Compare the results.